Seishin Shuyo

Seishin Shuyo

Mental Training in Traditional Martial Arts

James O. "Jimmy" Lockett

Cover Art by Henry Binerfa

SavKen Publishing
Las Vegas, Nevada

ISBN-13: 978-1980298076

DEDICATION

To all my teachers and students, past, present, and future.

CONTENTS

INTRODUCTION

Most people are aware that martial arts practice offers more than meets the eye. It has been widely shown that there are many benefits to martial study and training beyond purely self-defense, sport or even physical fitness and health. It is well known that there are powerful mental and emotional benefits as well.

More often than not however, the actual mental attributes themselves, as well as the specific methods to attain them are discussed in a somewhat nebulous manner. There is very little information that is explained in clear, specific ways regarding this aspect of the martial arts.

The purpose of this small volume is to serve as an introduction to the specific mental qualities and attributes that can be developed through training in the traditional martial arts, as well as some of the training methods used to actualize those qualities. The term used for this study in Okinawan/Japanese martial practice is *Seishin Shuyo* (精神修養), which can be translated as "mental training."

It is important to understand that, for the martial artist, or budoka (Japanese term for martial arts practitioner), these practices are just as specific, detailed and trainable as any of the physical techniques. The concepts, mind-sets, strategies, and disciplines have evolved over centuries and, though most are not well known to the general public, to the budoka they are considered an absolutely vital part of true martial arts training and development.

It is my sincere hope that this volume will serve to bring this information more to the fore and help both the novice and the professional gain a clearer, deeper understanding of this profoundly important aspect of the martial lifeway.

QUALITIES OF A BUDOKA

Thoughts are real, substantive actualities. Thus, they too have their effect on the fabric of the universe.

JOL

One of the things most universally expressed by students beginning in their martial practice, as well as by observers who don't study these arts, is that there seems to be a "certain something," a demeanor or bearing, that is easily noticeable in those who have trained for a very long time. There are qualities in the way martial artists seem to carry themselves, that mark them as somewhat different from the norm. These qualities can sometimes be very subtle, but they are always there.

While there are many such qualities, and some arts will bring out certain ones more than others, there are a few that show themselves again and again. The longer the person practices, the more deeply these qualities become ingrained and the more natural they feel and appear.

These attributes are the result, not only of intense physical training, but also of deep self-examination as well as commitment to the disciplines of Seishin Shuyo - the mental training and study practices of the martial way.

Some of the more universal qualities one will notice in a long-time martial artist, or budoka, are:

Unshakeable Calm
Clarity of Thought
Open Mind
Uninhibited Spirit
Compassionate Heart
Balanced Lifestyle
Indomitable Will

Unshakeable Calm

The budoka lives a life committed to a clearly defined fundamental purpose. That purpose serves as the rock on which the budoka stands in all situations. Essentially, the budoka knows what s/he is doing at all times - namely, living a lifestyle committed to study and training, aiming not only for preparedness but for excellence, and attempting to actualize his or her highest capabilities in the expression of the martial arts and ways. It has been said that one begins training in martial arts for self-*protection*, but one continues training for self-*perfection*.

As you practice the many disciplines and assimilate the ideologies of the budoka lifeway, they begin to pervade every aspect of life, evoking a profoundly calm centeredness that cannot be shaken. Certainly, you may at times leap for joy, or at other times share tears of sadness. Indeed, you may experience the rich interplay of all human emotions. The powerful center that comes from clarity of purpose and regular practice of the martial disciplines - physical training, study, mental exercises, lifestyle choices, and more - allows you the freedom to feel as deeply as possible. However, at your center there remains a deep river of calm, underlying all that you experience - an imperturbable serenity that, in time, spreads outward to affect all those around you in a way that brings to them a sense of security and comfort. This is an unmistakable indicator that one is in the presence of a true budoka.

Clarity of Thought

A life of physical, mental, and spiritual discipline has been shown throughout history to lead inexorably to a kind of fundamental power and clarity in thinking that is instantly recognizable and respected. In all circumstances, and under the greatest of stresses, the well-trained mind will unerringly assert its powers. Neither pain, fatigue, intense emotion, nor any other factor will significantly diminish the clarity and discernment of s/he who has daily practiced the disciplines of his or her chosen path. This mental faculty, the ability to penetrate the fog of chaotic circumstance and to perceive the clear path ahead, serves as a cornerstone on which the practitioner depends when the path grows more difficult as the journey continues.

Clarity of thought, in the budo (martial way) context, functions on many levels. The budoka embraces the considerable value not only of the intellect but also of intuition, creativity, and emotion, and readily employs all these faculties in his or her thought processes when and where appropriate. The budoka seeks to use all facets of learning and perception, of analysis and problem-solving, of decision-making and leadership in a clear, powerful manner. The most basic martial disciplines establish the foundation for this vital ability, and it is continually exercised in gradually richer and more powerful ways as the long journey on the road to self-actualization continues.

Open Mind

The true mark of the budoka at the highest level is the openness, flexibility, and adaptability of his or her mind. The martial way is a path of learning, seeing, feeling, and experiencing on all levels. In this regard, the capacity to perceive without judgment or preconception is, perhaps, the most fundamental prerequisite to true understanding. Consistent practice of the various budo disciplines trains the mind in powerful mental tools for the acquisition, retention, recall, and application of skills. Such practice also serves to develop a quality of openness and adaptability to the fluid unpredictability, not only of the physical engagement of contest or combat, but also of the various ever-changing circumstances of daily life.

For the longtime practitioner of the budo lifestyle, who has assimilated the fundamental principles underlying the path, and who has practiced the disciplines over an extended period, it seems natural and obvious to allow for all possibilities, in all things, at all times. There is simply no impulse to judgment, but rather a genuine, almost childlike openness to every experience. Once acquired, this natural, simple, open quality of mind is easily retained throughout life, no matter how much one learns or experiences. Many of the budo disciplines have been chosen or developed with the intent to train and assimilate this capacity.

Uninhibited Spirit

The budoka lifeway seeks to aid the follower in continually developing deeper self-knowing and self-acceptance. Through this process, you may begin to feel a sense of openness of expression based on your natural tendencies, rather than on externally imposed conceptions of that which is considered fitting or proper. Not only do you feel things more deeply, you are also free to express those feelings fully.

This is not to say that you are inconsiderate of the effects of your actions or words upon others. The nature of martial arts training is such that you are always sensitive to your circumstances. For the budoka however, the capacity to allow mind, body, and spirit to soar, to feel deeply, to express all that you experience in a genuine and natural way, to live in a state of inner and outer harmony based on understanding and acceptance of your true nature, is the ultimate aim of every practitioner of the budoka lifeway.

Compassionate Heart

One of the results of long-term practice of the martial disciplines as a lifeway rather than purely for physical gains, is a greatly increased level of awareness of and empathy with all people. This empathy awakens in varying degrees at different stages of the process of personal actualization and is marked by a continually evolving understanding of the ways of others. With this understanding can come greater tolerance and, ultimately, compassion.

Tolerance comes through the acceptance that your own way is not the only one, or even the "right" one. There are many ways to view life and to live it. We begin to see, in a deep and genuine way, that each of us must find and live our own truth. Our reactions to the choices of others changes profoundly. We lose our tendency to make judgments and, in all relationships, seek a clear understanding of all the many levels of thought and feelings that are inherent in any personal interaction.

As our sensitivity to emotional nuance develops, our capacity to understand the thoughts and feelings of others grows stronger and we cannot help but begin to feel a powerful awareness of the emotions of those whom we encounter. This sensitivity, this empathy, coupled with our understanding and open-minded acceptance, engenders compassion, a sincere caring for the needs and feelings of others, which can neither be denied nor ignored.

This is a genuine and profound experience, resulting not from any belief that you *ought* to be compassionate, but from the true empathic sensibility that emerges with time and committed practice of the disciplines. The very process of opening your heart to the path and surrendering yourself to its tenets paves the way for this awareness.

A practitioner of the martial lifeway, believing that all life is interconnected on some level, soon comes to the realization that a compassionate heart allows us to perceive and understand our own experiences as well as those of others. The more clearly you understand yourself, the easier it becomes to understand and be tolerant of, and show compassionate for someone else.

These two aspects of consciousness, self-awareness and other-awareness, feed on one another in a continually upward spiral. We see that all the experiences of others are just as meaningful to them as ours are to us. In time, the experiences of others become so real to us that we feel them as though they were our own. We begin to care deeply for others, and our actions, even our thoughts, reflect that caring. This, in the way of the budoka, marks the genuine evolution of the compassionate heart.

Balanced Lifestyle

The budoka employs the attributes of the martial path to create a life that brings all his or her capacities to light in a natural, harmonious way - a life that, in many ways, reflects nature in the intricate interplay of all its forces. How this manifests itself will, of course, vary from person to person. The personal style of the budoka will reflect the individual's natural tendencies. One budoka may live in simple, austere surroundings and practice his or her disciplines quietly and alone, while another may live in elegant luxury, and yet another in the deep forest, desert, or mountains.

Still, thoughtful and open-minded examination will reveal a common thread, regardless of personal style. A true follower of the martial way will invariably seek a balance of all aspects of Self, and that balance will be reflected quite clearly in his or her day-to-day lifestyle.

Indomitable Will

The choice to follow the martial path brings with it tremendous difficulties that test the very depths of commitment of body, mind, and spirit. All the teachings of the ancients attest to this.

The most difficult aspect of the journey is simply staying on the path. In the face of tremendous life change, of little understanding or support from loved ones, of loss of friends, job, relationships, of injury and illness, of tremendous temptations of every sort, of fear, doubt, rage, guilt, pain, and sheer fatigue, of the inability to see any progress, and the sheer daunting prospect of the infinite journey, how do we hold to our commitment? Yes, there are times of ecstatic joy; yes, there are various stages of understanding and even enlightenment; and yes, there may come a time, well-along in the journey, when you will have difficulty even imagining living any other way.

Still, the reality is that few remain on any path, truly

committed in every way, long enough to reap the indescribable rewards that accrue with such a choice. It is simply too hard a life for most. At the end of the day, when it is difficult to see and understand the what and the why much less the how of our path, we must rely on one thing to get us through. That is simply the unrelenting will to continue taking the next step on the path day after day.

The hallmark of the warrior is endurance. The most basic lesson on the path is that the race is won by those who endure. The capacity to persevere in the face of adversity is a matter not solely of the body, but equally, if not more, of the mind and heart. Some of the budo disciplines test mind, body, and spirit to their very limits. The purpose of this is to train the disciple to continue to strive, to develop the deep inner belief that you always have a bit more, that you can always take just one more step, and that the capacity to reach inside and find the drive to do so is a matter of will.

In martial arts training there is a phrase, "Seishin Tanren", which can be translated; "to forge the spirit (like a sword)." The study and practice of martial arts forges the self in the fire of the will like the finest sword. The budoka recognizes that this Indomitable Will is the bedrock on which rests the ability to live in accord with the principles of the path every day of his or her life. It is this power of will that serves when all else fails.

The Indomitable Will does not require understanding, faith, or love. It is not affected by doubt, fear, grief, or pain. The truly indomitable will simply *is*. When this attribute is assimilated at the deepest levels, then, whether in darkness or light, the most fundamental requirement of any path can be met: *the inner strength to stay on the path, come what may.*

STATES OF MIND

A true seeker lives with a mind constantly open, aware that wisdom may be found in any place at any time, and allowing that wisdom to find its way to him.

JOL

Let's look at some of the specific mental studies one would undertake in the practice of the martial arts and ways that lead to the actualization of the kinds of qualities we discussed in the previous chapter. Note that, throughout the book we will use terms from Okinawan/Japanese martial arts, which are the sources of many, though not all, of the concepts we will consider. Some of the ideas and methods date from other places, particularly India and China, and, when appropriate we will try to make the origins clear. Primarily though, we will use Japanese terminology. We will, of course, explain the terms as we go along.

THE THREE SPIRITS

Fukutsu no Seishin (Persevering Spirit)

If there is a single mental quality that can be said to be universal in every martial culture, in every time and place, it would be Fukutsu no Seishin, the Persevering Spirit – never give up, never quit, never say die. The heart of the martial way is based, first, last and foremost on the ability to continue through adversity of every kind.

At the most basic level, when under physical attack, through fear, pain and fatigue, the single most important requirement is simply not to give up. Martial arts disciplines, as with all military basic training, and even most sports, virtually from the very first day, are specifically designed to help the practitioner develop this attribute. There are literally hundreds of drills, tests and aphorisms used by teachers, and coaches in every art and culture based on this principle.

At a higher level, of course, the persevering spirit can be applied in all aspects of life and in every endeavor. Whatever life brings, whatever one's goals or beliefs, whatever the challenge, the budoka learns to approach it with the fundamental strength to carry through. A strength of heart and mind, and a will to continue to the end, no matter the difficulty, is derived directly from the mental training inherent in regular martial practice. Fukutsu no Seishin – Persevering Spirit: Without this, nothing else is possible.

Kanto no Seishin (Fighting Spirit)

This, while in many ways self-explanatory, is one of the most highly prized qualities in all martial arts. It is something more than just the will the endure, it is an inner drive that impels one to fight back, to fight hard against an attack in whatever form it may take.

It is sometimes assumed that this quality is inborn but, in the martial ways it has been shown, time and again, to be trainable. If a person is brought along progressively and motivated properly, almost anyone can find the fighting heart within.

Hissho no Seishin (Winning Spirit)

Beyond the capacity to endure and the heart to fight lies another facet of the budoka mindset - the will to win. The drive to seize the moment and move forward to achieve a goal in the face of resistance, whether from an opponent, in daily life, or within oneself, is a key quality that marks the budoka for life. To see one's self as a winner, and to act accordingly makes any person, martial artist or otherwise, stand out from the crowd.

MANY MINDS

In Japanese, the word *shin* (心) can be translated as mind, heart, or spirit depending on the context. With Seishin Shuyo, there is a wide range mental states that can be cultivated. In many cases, they are quite specific and can be developed through awareness, diligence and practice. Here we look at some of the 'many minds' of the budoka.

Shoshin (Beginner's Mind)

Shoshin is the state of mind (shin) of the beginner (sho). Open, willing and, indeed eager to learn, it is the mentality wherein the beginner is ready to receive the initial instruction transmitted by the teacher, and the advanced practitioner retains the openness that allows continued learning and growth. This mindset is essential for continuing to assimilate knowledge and to progress in the development of skills. The true budoka cultivates this vital mindset. The practitioner who loses Shoshin, the beginner's mind, whether by thinking s/he knows everything, or by judgmentalism regarding another who may be teaching, creates a barrier to his or her own progress.

Zanshin (Remaining/Prepared Mind)

Zanshin is the state of mind (shin), of relaxed alertness which remains 'steady and ready', even after having defeated one's opponent(s). It is a prolonged state of vigilance (zan) in readiness to cope with any event, such as a surprise attack from another direction, or any other potential reaction. Zanshin should be present before, during and after execution of a technique, and especially after successfully defending against a real-life attack. In training, many systems require that the martial artist remain in the finishing position for several seconds after completing a series of techniques. Other systems may practice a complete scan of one's environment at such times. Whatever the training method, the concept remains: *"When the battle is over, and the war is won, and all your foes have been vanquished, then is the time to tighten your helmet strings."*

Mushin (No Mind)

Mushin is the state of non (mu) mind (shin). It is a variously thought of as a mental state in which the mind is not fixed on anything in particular, or a state in which there is no thought at all. Also called "Munen" (non-thinking), or Mushin no Shin (mind of no-mind), it is described and practiced throughout both martial arts and Zen culture. Many martial arts have as part of their goal, the ability to enter into this mental state during the execution of their techniques and, ultimately, even in combat.

Mushin is utterly free from ego, anger, fear or expectation. In this mindset the practitioner allows any thoughts to pass like clouds in the sky, without following them. The unbound mind remains free to react at any time. Mushin is often described as "mizu no kokoro", literally a mind, or heart (kokoro) of water (mizu). In other words, a mind that can flow freely, like water, it can instantly adapt to the shape of whatever it encounters. Conversely, if the mind can remain calm and still like the surface of a lake, it becomes a mirror that accurately reflects the reality of things as they are, without the inaccuracies inherent in preconception or expectation.

Fudoshin (Immovable Mind)

Fudoshin is the mind (shin) which is unperturbed (fudo) by any adverse circumstance. A mind that cannot easily be swayed from its fundamental purpose or commitment. It is a mindset which nothing from outside can shake. Fudoshin is that inner strength which enables us to meet any situation without hesitating or losing our way.

An important distinction here is that, by immovable mind, we definitely do not mean rigid and inflexible in thinking or opinions. Fudoshin is a state of solidity and firmness, steadfastness in the face of the storm, an unshakeable strength of will under all circumstances.

Isshin (Single/Focused Mind)

Isshin means 'one mind.' It is a state of total focus on one thought or act. It is the ability to commit totally to the moment without the slightest hesitation and with no other restricting thought. Ishhin is considered a very powerful tool in the execution of martial arts techniques. Generally, it is considered to be a state one attains only momentarily. However, in that brief moment of total commitment, one can often achieve levels of power, of effectiveness, far beyond one's normal capabilities. In self-defense, as in life, there may come a moment when one must let go completely and give one's whole self to the moment. In these circumstance, Isshin, a totally single-focused mind, may be the only recourse, the only way to save the day.

Heijoshin (Unshakeable Calm Mind)

This is discussed in detail in the previous chapter. Here we explain the specific martial term for this quality. Hei (calm), jo (always), shin (mind) is the mentality of always remaining calm and centered in any situation. It is one of the hallmarks of the high level budoka.

Nyuunanshin (Open, Flexible Mind)

As above, one aspect of this mentality is also discussed

in the previous section, that being general open mindedness. With Nyu (flexible, pliable), nan (accepting), shin (mind), the main distinction here is that, in martial arts terms, Nyuunanshin refers specifically to the willingness to be taught. In this context, it's not really about trust or belief in a particular teacher or system, it's more about a mentality of willingness and acceptance of the idea of being taught.

One of the things the experienced budoka eventually becomes certain of is that s/he doesn't know everything. The methods, concepts, strategies, tactics and techniques are so vast that there is always more to learn. Further, there are many different, equally viable ways to perform even an individual technique.

The true budoka is always willing to learn, to be taught, to be shown. It is fundamental to the growth process and an integral aspect of the martial path. On many occasions you will find even the highest-level masters studying new material or taking classes from someone of a lower rank but in a different style. They can put aside, for the moment, their position and knowledge, open their minds and, through the nyuunanshin mindset, willingly allow themselves to be taught.

Yoshin (Flexible/Adaptible Mind)

Yoshin means, "willow mind or willow heart" and implics a quality of flcxing without brcaking, of adapting without losing one's essence or true nature. In practice, it is also the ability to switch quickly and effectively from one plan of action or technique to another as the situation requires, to abandon what is not working without attachment and immediately try a different option while still maintaining the original goal. Yoshin, is to yield with a purpose or to, "flow with the go." "*The most important thing in Kendo (Way of the Sword) is a flexible mind, which makes one humble enough to recognize one's own weakness and to overcome it through practice.*" Sensei Kenichi Ishida, 8th Dan, Kendo

Shingen (Compassionate/Understanding Mind)

In this context the word *shin* means, 'heart' or 'soul,' and *gen*, means, 'sight' or 'clairvoyance.' Thus, Shingen is the ability to perceive and understand the heart of another and/or to see deeply into the underlying forces of situations.

Kyushin (Circle Mind)

Kyushin is the mind that aids in avoiding or resolving conflicts. By viewing all sides of any situation and using words and body language in appropriate ways, one can employ 'circular forms' that blend the forces of Yin and Yang (In and Yo) to create harmony rather than discord.

Senshin (Shenshin) (Enlightened Mind)

Senshin is the mind (shin) which is purified or enlightened (sen) and transcends the other mind-sets. It is purified mind, free from everything that is not in harmony or "aï," and embraces all with empathic understanding and without ego. This state of muga (egolessness) brings the budoka into harmony with the All.

KIHON GEIKO – BASIC TRAINING

There are no secret techniques, no magic, no hidden knowledge. The whole answer is simple. Practice every day.

JOL

6 Japanese Words for Practice

In the Okinawan/Japanese martial arts there are six different words for training or practice. Each has a slightly different connotation and the combination of them forms a significant part of the mentality of the budoka trainee. The six words are:

Keiko (Study/Practice)

Renshu (Training)

Shuren or Shunren (Discipline)

Tanren (Forging)

Kufu (Long-Term Skill)

Shugyo (Personal Challenge)

Keiko (Study)

The word Keiko, (稽古) along with several variations, is an everyday word used for regular practice, training or study. It is the most standard word you will hear when referring to daily practice or study, winter or summer training, etc.

Renshu (Training)

Renshu (練習), is another every day word that refers more directly to the concept of training in the sense of repeating something again and again in order to learn it well. It also can connote classifying things into specific categories to help gain clarity in understanding.

*Shun*ren (Discipline)

Shunren (習練) in one form of kanji (Japanese written characters) is simply the reverse of the previous term renshu. However, there is more than one form of kanji for the term and each of them can have slightly different connotations. In general, Shunren refers to the mentality of acceptance of the slow, regular process of continually working, studying, practicing something for a very long time.

Tanren (Forging)

Tanren (鍛錬) implies the process of forging through continual hard work, of going through the fire, and of the beating of heated metal into a powerful, useful shape. The phrase Seishin Tanren – usually translated as "spirit forging," is a widely accepted concept in Okinawan and

Japanese martial arts. Many schools have various forms of training that use this term. Seishin Tanren means to forge mind, body, spirit, and technique, like a sword, through the fire of continuous hard training and diligent study.

Kufu (Long-Term Skill)

Kufu (功夫) implies developing excellence in the execution of any act through long term practice, dedicated study and deep thought. It also can have the implication of dedication to inner or spiritual improvement, particularly in relation to Zen meditation. Kufu (in Chinese pronounced Kung Fu) can refer to any skill attained through the long, consistent process of hard work, study, and practice.

Shugyo (Personal Challenge)

Shugyo (修行) is the process of challenging oneself by performing difficult tasks. The implication is that the intention is to deepen and refine one's character through the process of taking on challenges to mind, body, and spirit. Shugyo is often seen in the form of physical tasks such as a long pilgrimage on foot. However, the task can be mental as well, such as a type of meditation practice for an extended period or under difficult conditions (such as under a waterfall). Shugyo can be a single event, like running a marathon, or a task that takes many months or even years to complete.

KIHON

In every field there is a body of fundamental knowledge and skills which anyone undertaking that endeavor must learn. Without meeting these basic requirements, regardless of the particular subject, be it science, art, sport or philosophy, one simply cannot reach the highest levels of comprehension and performance. This is certainly true in the case of martial arts training in general, and of Seishin Shuyo (mental training) in particular.

The following section covers in a bit more detail, some of the most fundamental skills taught in traditional martial arts, which serve as the foundation on which higher level mental training is built. These techniques are called Kihon, which translates as basics.

There are physical kihon, basic techniques such as stances, footwork, falling, striking, cutting, etc., which the budoka practices endlessly throughout his or her lifetime in the arts. There are also mental kihon, specific exercises that prepare the mind for the rigorous training which is a necessary aspect of the martial way.

These kihon should be practiced with just as much diligence and consistency as the physical methods. Indeed, some might argue that the Seishin Shuyo Kihon Waza (Mental Training Basic Techniques) are far more important than the physical. Physical skill without mental development is an empty and, ultimately ineffective pursuit. For the budoka, both are considered equal and are given their due in daily practice.

Kihon I – Kokyu Ho (Breath Control)

The art and science of breath control is one of the most fundamental and powerful tools one can acquire in the quest for personal actualization. Throughout history, it has been shown that the capacity to consciously direct the flow of breath is a vital aspect of enhanced performance in an incredibly broad range of areas. From the purely physical to the deeply metaphysical, indeed in every area of human endeavor, it seems that the conscious control of breathing serves as the very first of the keys to power. Understanding and practicing breath control will confer greater health and longevity upon the body, sharpen and clarify the workings of the mind, and facilitate the actualization of deeper spiritual awareness.

A wide variety of methods of breath control have evolved over the centuries to meet the needs and priorities of different cultures. In the East, such practices as the Taoist energy conservation techniques, the Indian pranayama, the Chinese chi-kung or the Japanese kokyu waza are but a few. In the Western world, virtually every activity - from a variety of sports, ranging as widely as swimming, gymnastics, shooting and other physically demanding activities, to therapeutic methods of stress management and relaxation - has an appropriate breathing method. As an example, every trained singer in the Western world spends a major portion of his or her efforts on the development and maintenance of good breath control. Without it, one simply cannot sing well. Even so "natural" an act as childbirth is taught with breathing techniques as an integral aspect of the bringing forth of new life. Virtually any physical activity that requires strength, endurance, coordination, power, balance, speed, fluidity, and mental acuity, is directly affected by proper (or improper) breathing.

While there exists an immense variety of specialized breathing methods, most can be said to be based on certain principles. The techniques discussed here are derived from the most basic and universal of those principles. They are intended to serve as an introduction to and a foundation upon which more activity-specific breath control methods may be based. These techniques are quite simple. The most important requirement is daily practice.

Fukushiki Kokyu (Diaphragmatic Breathing)

The most basic and widely accepted controlled breathing method is known as diaphragmatic breathing. The technique is based on the natural action of the diaphragm, a convex band of muscle extending across the entire chest cavity from front to back (like an upside-down bowl) just beneath the lungs and separating the chest cavity from the abdominal cavity. During inhalation, the diaphragm flexes, flattening somewhat and pressing downward thus allowing the lungs to expand. During exhalation, the diaphragm returns to its original concave position, pushing air out of the lungs. While there are several accessory muscles involved in breathing - in particular the internal and external intercostals-and many other factors that affect both inspiration and expiration, the diaphragm is the prime mover and the one with which we are most concerned. As all muscles contract in only one direction, the diaphragm cannot "flex" upward. What is possible, however, is to control both the degree and the rate of downward flexion and upward relaxation, thus controlling the flow of breath.

The most obvious effect of such conscious control is the ability to affect the amount of oxygen entering the lungs and therefore the bloodstream, as well as the rate of carbon dioxide leaving the body. This clearly can affect the function of the body's various systems.

Somewhat less obvious may be effects such as your level of physical relaxation, heart rate, muscular tension, mental clarity, response to stress, emotional state, concentration, and sensitivity to your surroundings.

Basic Breath Control Exercises

The following exercises will help develop skill in the use of diaphragmatic breathing techniques and establish a strong foundation for higher level breath control skills. It cannot be over-emphasized that daily practice is necessary for any real effectiveness to be realized. The secret to success in any endeavor is consistency over time. Practicing a discipline regularly over a period of many years has a totally different effect than just a few weeks, or even several months of practice. One must learn to think in terms of years - really, of a lifetime - of regular practice.

The disciplines of your chosen path must be incorporated into daily life in a natural, harmonious way. This is the secret of the ancestors, and one of the true keys to self-actualization.

Exercise 1: Proper breathing starts with good posture. Stand or sit comfortably with the spine erect. The head rests naturally upon the spine, tilted neither up nor down. The spine retains its natural curves with a sense of erectness without tension. Lift the sternum (the flat, central bone of the upper chest where the ribs attach) gently, as if a string is attached to the center of your chest and someone is pulling it upward toward the ceiling. Try to hold this raised position throughout the breathing cycle. This allows the lower torso to expand more completely upon inhalation, making for increased tidal volume; that is, the amount of air taken in during one inspiration. Inhale slowly through the nose for about four medium-speed counts. While inhaling, allow the lower abdominal area to expand gently. Do not try to hold the abdominal muscles in. Remember that the diaphragm is shaped like an upside down bowl that flattens downward as you breathe in. As the diaphragm pushes down, it will tend to push the abdominal section outward due to the pressure exerted on the internal organs. Resisting this, holding the abdominal muscles in, limits the depth of inhalation, thereby diminishing the overall effectiveness of the technique.

After a complete inhalation, exhale gently and smoothly through the mouth. There are several important points to remember while exhaling. Most importantly, exhale evenly. There is a strong tendency to exhale the greater portion of air during the first second or two. DO NOT ALLOW YOURSELF TO DO THIS. The goal is to expend the same amount of air in the last second as in the first. Throughout the duration of exhalation, a steady, even amount of air should flow. When it becomes impossible to sustain a steady, even breath, it is time to stop and inhale once more. It is a little difficult to manage at first but is an absolute requirement. This is the first area wherein one begins to develop genuine breath control.

During exhalation, allow the abdominal muscles to gently fall inward. Do not push. There are many methods of exhaling, including pushing in strongly, pushing in softly, holding the abdominal muscles in the extended position while exhaling, pushing with the upper, middle, or lower abdominals, and many more. (All of these techniques have value, and generally serve a specific purpose. An in-depth study of the various breathing methods is highly recommended and will prove well worth your efforts. For our purposes, the most basic natural method will serve to establish the proper foundation.) Allowing the abdominal section to fall naturally inward is the normal response to the relaxation of the diaphragm as it returns to its inverted-bowl shape and the abdominal pressure is relieved.

There will probably be a tendency toward longer exhalation than inhalation. For this exercise, allow the timing to flow naturally. Inhale to a medium-speed four-count, and exhale until there is no more support to sustain a full amount of breath. Do not attempt to force the lungs to completely expend all of the air they contain. Complete exhalation is a more advanced technique that will be encountered in independent study.

As you exhale, the mouth should be only slightly opened and the air blown out in a controlled manner, almost like whistling. Many disciplines teach that the tip of the tongue should be held touching the roof of the mouth. If your studies indicate this, then you should do so. The lips, however, should be relaxed rather than tensed.

When the sense of support, the feeling that one can expend the same amount of breath continuously, is lost, it is time to inhale once more. Try to make the transition between inhale/exhale and between exhale/inhale as smooth as possible.

Start with four "sets" of four complete cycles (one inhalation and one exhalation = one cycle, four cycles = one set). Practice twice daily, once upon waking and once before going to sleep. Gradually increase the number of cycles to ten. When four sets of ten cycles twice daily becomes comfortable progress to the next exercise.

The following exercise is intended as a fundamental discipline. This technique and its variations should be thought of as forming the basis of one's breath control development and should become a lifelong daily practice.

Exercise 2: Using the breathing method described in exercise one, inhale while mentally counting to four. The speed should be approximately one count per second.

After inhaling hold the breath for four counts. When holding the breath it is important to remain as relaxed as possible. Avoid tensing the body. Simply hold the breath gently for the proper amount of time, then softly release it.

After holding for four counts, exhale smoothly also counting four. In this exercise the intention is not only to sustain an equal amount of breath during exhalation but to control the amount of time it takes to complete an exhalation. Performed properly, the end of four counts should coincide exactly with the feeling that it is time to inhale once again.

The transitions between inhalation, holding, and exhalation should be as smooth as possible. There should be a sense that no particular action is taking place to cause the holding or the exhaling. Each stage of the breathing cycle should occur easily and naturally.

After exhaling to a count of four inhale once again. This entire cycle, inhale four counts, hold four counts, exhale four counts, should be executed four times.

Upon completion of a set of four cycles of the above four count exercise move immediately, with no break in the flow, to a set of the six-count version of the same exercise. That is; inhale six counts, hold six counts, exhale six counts. This cycle should be repeated six times. Then move, again with no break in the flow, to a set of the eight-count version: inhale eight counts, hold eight counts, exhale eight counts; repeat eight times. Make sure that you don't speed up your rate of counting. Maintain a rate of about one count per second.

Finally perform nine complete nine-count breaths with no holding. Inhale for a count of nine and smoothly, and under control, exhale for a count of nine. Do this nine times. It is all important that the exhalation remain under control and of equal intensity through the whole nine counts.

This is quite a difficult exercise. It is unlikely that anyone without previous training will be able to execute it completely and properly at first. Daily practice will be required. The aim is the ability to execute the entire exercise smoothly and in a relaxed manner without a break. When this is accomplished one may feel that the first step on the road to breath control has been taken.

Summary: The 4/6/8 exercise

1. inhale 4 counts, hold 4 counts, exhale 4 counts, repeat 4 times
2. inhale 6 counts, hold 6 counts, exhale 6 counts, repeat 6 times
3. inhale 8 counts, hold 8 counts, exhale 8 counts, repeat 8 times
4. inhale 9 counts, exhale 9 counts, repeat 9 times

For these basic exercise remember to inhale through the nose, exhale through the mouth. There are other patterns you will learn through further study but this is the basic method.

Variations: (after six months practice of 4/6/8 exercise.)

1. Change ratios of inhalation or holding.
    a. 2-2-4, 3-3-6, 4-4-8 (counts)
    b. 4-2-4, 6-3-6, 8-4-8
    c. 1-4-4, 1-6-6, 1-8-8 etc.
2. Change speed of counting. (faster or slower)
3. Add visualization of selected images and/or colors for each cycle.
4. Add vocalization of selected sound(s) during exhalation.
5. Execute while in motion. Start with walking back and forth, progress to various forms of movement.

Each of the above variations have specific aims which the reader can explore through independent study.

ıūchū (Concentration)

.. the process of personal development, whether in education, physical or mental achievement, business, artistic expression, or spiritual growth – indeed, in any human endeavor - the most important tool one must acquire is concentration. The ability to focus your attention and maintain that focus for the duration of any task, be it short, or long-term, is the ultimate determinant of the level of your attainment.

Fortunately, this vital faculty is completely trainable. Further, you can develop this skill at any age. Ideally, you would start to develop the skills and habit of concentration in early childhood, through games and exercises constructed as play. Even at a very advanced age, however, you can develop this powerful tool with relatively simple exercises. The key is consistent practice.

Let us first define concentration for the purposes of this study. Concentration is the ability to focus attention and to maintain that focus at will. We need to be clear that while there can be more than one way to explore any subject, for our purposes, we are dividing the concept of concentration into two distinct skills: *focusing* attention, and *maintaining focus* (sometimes called vigilance). Our training must be oriented toward developing both of these, in order to actualize effective powers of concentration.

The first step in this process is to understand some very basic principles. The most important principle to absorb in the study of concentration is that tension works against concentration. Many people view concentration as something requiring tension. You hear terms like "concentrating hard" or "intensely focused," usually implying that one is working with furious intensity. This image may be a product of our socialization concerning the virtues of "hard work." In fact, achieving a high level of concentration requires that you relax as much as possible. The more tension you bring to the task, the less energy left to focus on your subject.

This leads to the next principle of concentration, that of *doing* rather than *trying to do*. The harder you try, the more you are focused on the act of trying to concentrate, rather than actually being focused on your subject. In short, in order to achieve a high level of concentration, you must relax, and not try.

There are different levels of concentration appropriate to different types of tasks. In budoka training, we recognize three levels of concentration, which exist as ranges, from low to high. Within each of these there are variations determined by your intentions. This breakdown is mostly a matter of convenience, and others might choose a different but equally valid approach. The levels of concentration as studied in the budoka way are:

Level I - General Focus: used for regular practice and study, projects, reading, organization of information, etc.

Level II - High Level: kata (preset forms) practice, memorization (particularly long-term), complex analysis, intense creative work, focusing perceptions.

Level III - High Intensity (near-total): total momentary

commitment, deep meditation, hypermnesia (total sensory recall).

The ability to achieve and maintain such levels of concentration, at will, may be the single differentiating factor between dreaming and realizing those dreams.

Finally, there are various factors that can affect our ability to concentrate. Some examples include: level of fatigue, emotional state, environment, internal distractions (hunger, pain, physical discomfort), or even the nature of the task itself. We are all aware that it is easier to focus on things we find interesting or meaningful than on those we find meaningless, distasteful, or simply boring.

Our aim, however, is to develop the ability to focus our mental powers at will. If we can control these extraneous factors then it will certainly be to our advantage. But skill in concentration can be developed to the degree that, despite external influences, little short of a life threat would serve to distract from your focus.

The following exercises will help begin the process of developing powers of concentration. As in the first Kihon, and with all those that follow, the most important thing is consistent practice over an extended period. These are beginner-level exercises. After working with them for a time, you will want to seek studies that will take you to continually higher levels.

Exercise 1: Counting - This exercise is very easy to understand and very difficult to perform. It should be practiced immediately upon completion of Kihon I.

After completing the breath-control exercise, breathe comfortably for a few moments. While maintaining a smooth flow of breath, begin counting in your mind. The exercise is simple: your goal is to count mentally from one to ten. As you count, however, if you have any thought whatsoever other than the counting, you must start over. We must emphasize that anything that touches your conscious awareness must be considered a distracting thought, and you must start over.

Clearly, only you will truly know what is in your mind, so it is easy to cheat if you so choose! The degree of your attainment of skill in concentration will be directly proportional to your diligence and self-honesty in this exercise.

If you reach the point where you can consistently count to ten without the intrusion of a single distracting awareness, then continue your counting to gradually higher numbers, adding five at a time - aim next toward fifteen, then twenty, and so on. If you ever reach the point where you can consistently count to one hundred without a single distracting thought, then you may consider yourself well on the road to strong powers of concentration.

Exercise 2: Object Focus - This can be practiced whenever you find a convenient few moments. Take a simple object in hand, such as a pencil, a comb, or a small stone. After a few relaxing breaths, note the time. Focus your attention on the object you are holding. Note everything about it - shape, color, texture, smell, unique features, etc. Focus all of your senses totally on the object. After a time, you will notice yourself thinking of other things or becoming distracted in one way or another. Note the time. How long were you able to maintain your focus?

Next, evaluate the exercise. Were you able to bring your attention completely to the object? Were all of your senses involved? Can you remember moments of distraction or lack of focus that occurred earlier than your noted time? Why were you distracted? Did your mind wander to other associations? Were there physical distractions such as discomfort, or external factors in the environment? Can something be done about these to aid in your ability to focus your attention and maintain that? Set simple goals to gradually increase the length of time and degree of your immersion in whatever object you choose to focus.

Exercise 3: Mental Focus - This is performed in exactly the same manner as Exercise 2, with the exception that the focus object is in your mind rather than your hands. It is usually easier to start this by mentally focusing on something already used as a focus subject in Exercise 2. The ultimate intent is to develop the ability to bring to mind any object, such as a cat or tree, and mentally examine it in detail without losing your focus. The same evaluation process that was used in the previous exercise should be performed upon completion.

Exercise 4: - This is best practiced with a training partner, although there are solo versions. Sit facing your partner. At an agreed-upon signal, both of you begin speaking at the same time. Describe something about yourself or an event about which you are certain your partner knows nothing. Use as much detail as possible including specific dates, times, names, as well as clear descriptions of persons, places, or objects. Continue this for approximately one minute. Afterwards, take turns describing everything you remember each other saying. The objective is to hold your train of thought while hearing as much as possible of what your partner says. As you get better at this, you can increase the length of time of the exercise, the level of detail, or even add a third participant. For the solo version of this exercise, you can use a television or radio with a recorder as your partner. Find something informative on television or radio and let it play aloud while you are speaking aloud. Be sure to record the television or radio program. Test yourself against the recording to determine how much material you were able to digest while talking.

To add an element of difficulty to this version of the exercise, instead of talking, read aloud while recording the television or radio. The more information-dense the reading material and the recorded program, the more difficult the exercise. Test yourself on the quantity and accuracy of your memory on the reading material as well as that which you recorded.

There are many different types of concentration exercises. You may even create your own, in time. The key concept is that concentration is one of the fundamental tools in any process of learning and growth. Thus, it is one at which you must work diligently, to develop to the highest level of which you are capable. The return on your investment of time and energy, as you progress to the more difficult stages of your journey, will be incalculable.

Kihon III - Shikaku-ka (Visualization)

In the process of seeking to use the skills you develop through training of mind, body, and spirit, one of the most effective tools you can employ is visualization. The ability to create clear, powerful mental representations of your intentions is one of the major steps in actualizing your dreams.

Virtually all great accomplishment begins with a vision. That vision is then nurtured and reinforced until, through the action of various principles and practices, it begins to develop a kind of self-perpetuating power. If the vision is strong enough, clear enough, and consistently reinforced, little can impede its eventual actualization. Sooner or later, vision becomes reality.

Like most of the methods we will discuss, visualization is a skill you develop through practice. You have read that visualization is the key to actualization. Few, however, have the ability to visualize clearly and reliably without training. It is a case of knowing what to do, but not how to do it.

Visualization presumes a few basic prerequisites. First, you need the ability to focus your mind, and maintain that focus (concentration). That skill is, of course, the subject of the previous Kihon. You must also understand a few simple concepts.

Visualization is the ability to create a clear, well-focused image in the mind. You must first realize that, in some ways, the term "visualization" is a bit of a misnomer. A clear mental image, in order to be most effective, must in fact, not only be visual, but must engage *all* of the senses. Thus, true visualization is not exclusively visual. The more senses such as touch, taste, smell, and hearing you can engage in your mental image, the more powerful it becomes.

Visualization training therefore must develop not only the inner eye, but all inner senses as well. Many people have trouble with the concept that you can visualize a smell, for example, but after a little reflection you realize that there are many smells you may have encountered-some good, some not-that can easily be recalled. One of the important keys to visualization is to use this faculty, the ability to recreate sensory experiences, to engage all your senses in the process of creating visualizations.

Another important factor is clarity. You must work toward the ability to create crystal - clear, sharp images with color, texture, crisp, clean sound, rich taste and smell, and full depth of dimension. A practitioner skilled in this craft can create visualizations of such total sensate richness that the mind can hardly differentiate them from "reality." When images attain this level of clarity, they become so powerful that they begin to become self-perpetuating.

Finally, you must be able to sustain the image you create. This is the key to manifestation. Clearly developed, richly detailed, multi-sensory visualizations, nurtured and maintained over time, begin to affect not only the mental plane on which they came into being, but also the actions of their creator. The vision becomes so powerful that you are moved to take the steps to bring that vision into reality.

The exercises below are the first steps on the road to developing the ability to create clear, effective visualizations. They are designed to help you acquire the basic tools necessary to practice this powerful skill. At this point, it may seem unnecessary to reiterate the importance of regular, consistent practice - but we will continue to repeat, ad nauseam, that the secret to success is consistency over time.

Exercise 1. Primary Colors - Upon completion of the breathing and counting exercise in the Kihon II, begin the following exercise. With eyes closed, imagine a small red dot in the center of your inner vision. Allow the dot to gradually increase in size until it fills your entire visual field. Imagine that this color red is moving toward you, filling all space until it sweeps through and past you. Try to perform the exercise in such a manner that you see nothing in your vision but the deep, rich color. After the color has swept past, imagine that the small dot has been replaced by the color yellow, which also expands to fill your visual field, moves toward you, and sweeps through and past you. Perform the same exercise with the color blue. Take your time with this exercise. Work on it until you can firmly envision the colors, and absolutely nothing else, in your mind's eye.

Exercise 2. Field Expansion - While performing the above exercise, eventually try to widen your visual field so that you seem to see further and further to your sides as well as upward and downward. Your mental vision is not limited in the same way as your physical vision. Try to train yourself to see further and further until you can see to the sides, above and below, and eventually in a complete circle simultaneously. This is often a difficult conceptual leap because you are imposing the limits of your body onto your mind. Remember: there are no such limits on the mental plane. Circular or even spherical vision is entirely possible, if you can break the habits imposed by the physical world and make the mentally free yourself from the restriction of a one-dimensional landscape to a true omni-dimensional mind-scape.

Exercise 3. Shapes and Sizes - As your powers of mental conceptualization become stronger, try expanding the dot on your inner screen into specific shapes. Make these as clear as possible, and don't allow yourself to cheat by accepting different shapes than you intended. The goal here is to develop the power to control your visualizations as completely as possible, and to use that skill in your practical world. Start with basic shapes - triangle, square, circle - and expand the size, change the color, position, angle, and motion of the chosen shape. Work for complete control. As you grow stronger, you may work with more complex shapes in more difficult configurations. You may add more than one shape, but the decisions must always be intentional on your part.

Exercise 4. Multiple Senses - Finally, try to bring your other senses into play in your inner visualizations. Give your shapes not only color, but texture as well. Try to develop your inner sense of touch in the same way as your inner vision. Change the texture and temperature, as well as other tactile qualities of your focus object, and feel them with your mental body. Do this as well with your other senses, hearing, taste, and smell. Keep in mind that your inner senses are not limited in the same ways as your external ones. Imagine such broader perceptions as the sound of a color and the taste of a sound. Blend and use your senses in as many new ways as you can imagine. Continued work on these exercises will lead to tremendously powerful and effective use of visualization as a tool to assist you on your journey.

Kihon IV – Meisō (Meditation)

In every discipline, there will usually be a fundamental tool, a basic required practice or skill, without which the highest levels of attainment cannot, under most circumstances be achieved. In the world of music, we hear of the endless practice of scales and fingering, in ballet, the barre and stretching-in every endeavor where great skill or knowledge is required, there will be the most basic of drills. For the seeker of true self - actualization through the martial ways, one of the most fundamental skills is meditation.

In every culture throughout human history that has engaged in practices intended to enhance the powers of mind, body, or spirit, some form of meditative training can be found. Of all the tools available to the seeker, there is none that can more reliably evoke the transcendence of limiting conception, the perception of universal principles, and the personal mystical experience.

There are, of course, many forms of meditation, and in fact many differing and often conflicting conceptions of what, exactly, meditation is. By now, you may have perceived that, from the budoka point of view, all forms of practice may be worthwhile. There is no single "right" method of meditation. Each form of practice has developed to serve the needs and beliefs of those who practice it.

Unfortunately, even people who practice meditation regularly often don't have a real understanding of its broad ranging nature and variety of methods. The most important concept is that meditation is a skill that requires practice of specific drills which must be developed to a very high level before true meditation can be practiced consistently.

In the martial ways there are several types of meditation and they can form a very dynamic and powerful practice. Many of the techniques are very specific and, in some of their forms, quite technical. The purpose of this is to develop the powers of mind to their highest, to engender the fusion of the mental, physical, and spiritual into one, to engage that totality at its highest level of function, and to catalyze the processes that may bring about the actualization of our untapped potential.

An examination of the many techniques of meditation will show that there are certain aspects common to virtually all of them. It is these commonalities, combined with methods specific to our particular needs, that serve as the foundation for the budoka approach to this vital skill. In the following explanation and exercises we will focus on seated meditation. To be sure, meditation while in motion is also a part of martial practice, however, this section is devoted to Kihon, the basics, so we begin at the beginning.

Meditation generally consists of seven successive steps:

1. Posture
2. Quieting the mind
3. Breath control or awareness
4. Strengthening or protecting visualization
5. Meditation
6. Release - reorientation - expression of gratitude
7. Post-meditation stretch

Clearly, a complete course in meditation is impractical to describe here; however, by following the format explained below, the student can make a solid beginning. It is step number 5 above, the meditation itself, that we must now, however briefly, consider.

For the sake of clarity, we can categorize types of meditation into four separate classes:

Inquisitive Meditation - seeks an answer or conclusion. The Inquisitive class of meditation has three forms:

Analytic, where you focus on a particular concept and, through one of various methods, attempt to discern its essence;

Associative, similar to analytic except in the methods used to explore the subject;

Intuitive, where you seek, through any of a wide variety of techniques, to bring about intuitive, non-rationalized leaps of awareness or comprehension.

Affirmative Meditation - expresses or affirms an experience, belief, or ideal. The intention is to bring that ideal into being in your psyche or material reality, through repeated and focused affirmation.

Insensible Meditation - seeks experience of the void, nothingness. D.T. Suzuki, a well-known author on Zen writes: *"When the mind has been so trained as to be able to realize a state of perfect void in which there is not a trace of consciousness left, even the sense of being unconscious having departed; in other words, when all forms of mental activity are swept away clean from the field of consciousness, leaving the mind like the sky devoid of every speck of cloud, a mere broad expense of blue, Dhyana* (the meditative state) *is said to have reached its perfection."*

Contemplative Meditation - seeks complete immersion and identification of Self as one with the subject or object of focus.

In the budoka meditative practice, you decide in advance which form of meditation you intend to attempt and, through regular daily practice, work toward the ability to consistently immerse yourself totally in the experience of that practice. Thus, any subject and method may require weeks or even months of practice before you move on. The method and subjects are chosen for the developmental effect they will have at that stage of the seeker's practice.

A typical budoka meditation would entail:

A. Finding a quiet space and sitting comfortably either in a chair, cross-legged, or lotus fashion, with the spine erect
B. Initiating a series of "visualization" exercises designed to quiet the mind
C. The 4-6-8 breath-control exercise, coupled with healing visualization and concentration techniques
D. A protecting and/or strengthening visualization
E. The predetermined meditation itself

F. Release from the meditation exercise, and internal expression of gratitude
G. A brief post-meditation physical stretch or light movement series to bring the body smoothly back to normal, comfortable motion

This entire process could take anywhere from 20 minutes to an hour or more, depending on the experience level and needs of the practitioner.

There are several important guidelines you ought to observe when attempting to meditate consistently, including:

- ❖ Remember the three P's: Patience, Perseverance, Practice.
- ❖ It's a good idea to determine in advance the preferred duration of the session. Some people use a gentle bell or other sound to tell when that time has expired.
- ❖ Never meditate half-heartedly. Commit yourself completely to each session.
- ❖ Your pre, and post-meditation attitude are very important. Try to carry as much positive energy and sincerity into your practice as possible. Also, try to carry the relaxed openness from your completed session with you when you're done.
- ❖ As mentioned earlier, it's usually best to decide on the subject and method you will use in

advance. This is not always necessary but is a good general practice.

- To derive the greatest benefit, it is usually better to work with a given subject over several sessions.
- Some people find aids such as music, candles, incense, quite helpful. You might also develop a pre-meditation ritual to help pre-set your mind for the upcoming session.
- It's best to avoid food at least an hour before meditation.
- Loose comfortable clothing is best.
- Some people find gentle stretching before (and definitely after) meditation to be quite helpful.
- If your meditation is interrupted briefly, try to retain a relaxed, calm state, and simply return to your practice as soon as possible, picking up where you left off. By "brief" we mean a few seconds or minutes at most. Any longer, and you will likely need to start again at another time.
- If possible, practice your meditation in the same place and around the same time each day. The best choice is a place used specifically and solely for that purpose, but for most of us this is not practical. However, using the same place every time will help to more easily achieve the meditative state.
- Avoid meditating when sleepy or over-tired.
- Avoid drugs or alcohol while meditating

❖ Study the many forms of meditation, through classes and media. Remember, there is no one-and-only "right" way to meditate.

Meditation is a foundation skill. It is one of the required tools for any who consider themselves truly serious about self-actualization. The astute reader may have perceived that the previous Kihon; Breath Control, Concentration, and Visualization passages have been incorporated into this practice. That is intentional. By following Kihon I - IV in succession, the student will build a firm ground on which to erect the cornerstones which will serve in his or her continuing journey. One of the most important of those cornerstones is the daily practice of meditation.

The list of subjects upon which you can meditate is literally infinite. Following are just a few such subjects. A subject may be used only once, or many times. You may also choose certain meditation subjects based on specific goals or life circumstances. In short, all things are potential subjects for meditation. As well, you may choose to meditate on no-thing. The following, are typical subjects often used in the formal study of meditation.

OM

Birth

Order

The beautiful bird gets caged

Mushin

Death

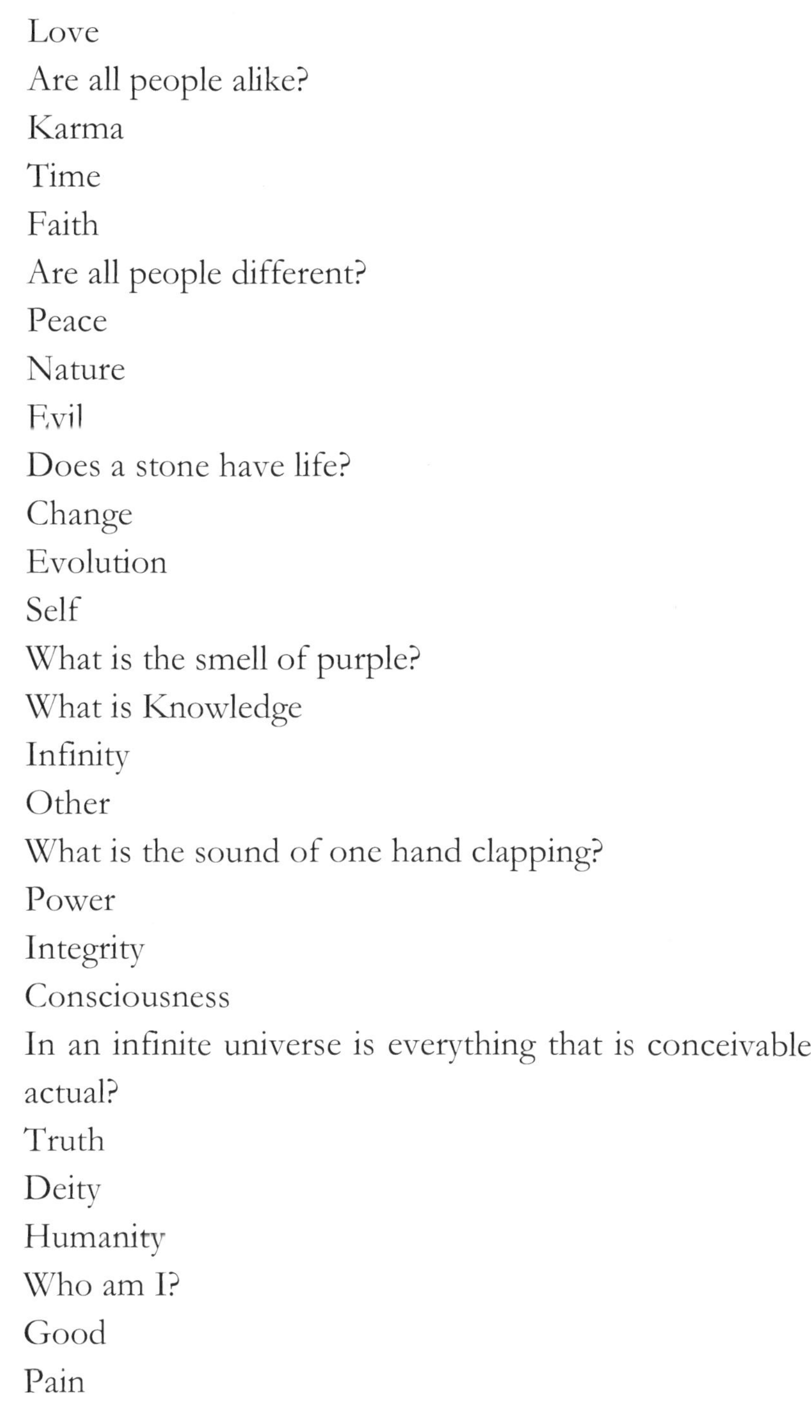

Love
Are all people alike?
Karma
Time
Faith
Are all people different?
Peace
Nature
Evil
Does a stone have life?
Change
Evolution
Self
What is the smell of purple?
What is Knowledge
Infinity
Other
What is the sound of one hand clapping?
Power
Integrity
Consciousness
In an infinite universe is everything that is conceivable actual?
Truth
Deity
Humanity
Who am I?
Good
Pain

Life
What is Freedom?
Form
Patience
Meaning
What is self-actualization?
Empty your cup
Formlessness
Water
Oneness
Thoughts are things
Blue
Value
Eternity
All is one

Clearly, there are far too many meditation exercises to list here, or in any single volume. The following contains one example from each of the four classes of meditation listed above. You are strongly encouraged to study meditation in greater detail.

1. Inquisitive (Associative form) - Choose, in advance, the subject upon which you intend to practice your meditation exercise. After completing the first four steps described above-posture, quieting the mind, breath control, protecting visualization - bring the subject you have chosen into your mind. Allow your subject simply to exist - don't try to do anything with it. In a short time, you will notice

another thought has come to mind, perhaps related to the subject in some way, or perhaps not in any way that you can discern. Allow yourself to become aware of the new thought for a moment. Do not examine it or follow it. Simply notice. Then bring your mind back to the original subject and focus your attention. Soon, another association will come to mind. Again, simply notice without taking action; after a moment, return to your original subject. Continue this process again and again - subject, association, back to subject - until you feel yourself becoming mentally fatigued, or you notice yourself tending to follow your associations rather than returning to your central subject, or until the time you have allotted for meditation expires. Release your mind from your chosen subject with a positive sense of gratitude. Move on to the post-meditation stretch. Take a few moments afterward to consider the various associations that came to you during your practice. You may find that some very interesting and surprising issues for further consideration can emerge from this exercise.

2. Affirmative - Choose a subject that you wish to affirm deeply in your psyche. An example might be a phrase such as "I embrace my inner nature," or "Good is never lost." Follow the routine of steps 1 – 4, as described above. Upon reaching the meditation portion of the practice, bring your affirmation into your conscious mind. Employing your skill of visualization, state your affirmation in such a way that all your inner senses-hearing, vision, taste, touch, smell - are engaged. After stating your affirmation, state another

sentence as an example that your affirmation is true. The meditation might proceed in a manner similar to: "Good is never lost. This is the principle of Karma. Good is never lost. Even when you don't see the results, they still exist. Good is never lost. It moves outward like the ripples in a pond. Good is never lost…" and so on. Continually return to your original affirmation and allow a confirming thought to flow from there. Again, continue until the exercise feels complete. Release the subject with joy and gratitude. Post - stretch.

3. Insensible - The objective of this form of meditation is to experience nothingness, the Void, no mind, no thoughts, no awareness whatsoever. There are so many approaches to this form of meditation that even to make a serious beginning would require a volume in itself. In the following exercise, you will follow the same procedure as described previously in steps 1 - 4. Next, relax and allow yourself to become aware of each of your senses in turn. First, focus on your body and all your physical sensations. Next, on sound, smell, and taste. With each sense, try to hold full awareness of one as you move to the next. In other words, once you become fully aware of your body, try to retain that awareness as you focus on hearing, then retain both as you focus on smell, then taste. Your aim is to become complete engaged in all of your senses simultaneously. When you reach the level that you can hold onto this awareness, use your powers of visualization to gradually shrink that awareness into a ball that grows smaller and

smaller until it becomes a tiny dot. Then allow the dot to vanish into grayness. Rest in that space of gray nothingness until you become aware of your Self. Release the meditation with positiveness and gratitude. Post - stretch.

4. Contemplative - Choose a physical object, as you would in the Concentration exercises in the Kihon II. Before your session, focus your mind completely on that object. Look at it. Touch it, smell it, taste it, tap it and listen. Become as familiar with every aspect of the object as you can. After following steps 1 - 4 of the now, hopefully, familiar meditation sequence, bring your focus object into your thoughts. Take a little time to review your previous experience of it with all your inner senses. Gradually, allow yourself to sink your awareness into the focus object. Rather than what the object feels like - is it rough or smooth, hot or cold - you want to begin to feel as if you are the object. Perceive the world as if you were the object you are focusing on. What do you feel from the inside? More than just intellectually speculating on what it might be like, allow yourself to become the object of your focus so completely that Self-as-human is overcome by Self-as-object. With practice, you may be able to achieve this level of identification, not only with physical objects, but with concepts, forces of nature, or even other living beings. The essence of this practice is total surrender, and thus total immersion, leading to total awareness.

Kihon V – The Inner Sanctum

The following exercise is a powerful and effective tool that has a wide range of uses in the process of self-actualization. You should begin working on this only after practicing the exercises in Kihon I through IV for a minimum of several weeks.

Find a quiet comfortable place where you will not be disturbed for at least half an hour. You may sit in a meditation position or, if you prefer, you may use a comfortable chair, or lie down. Do not perform this exercise if you so tired that you are likely to fall asleep.

Close your eyes and perform the basic four-breaths exercise. Allow yourself to relax as completely as possible. Take some time to note, and release, points of tension throughout your body. After some time, become aware of a sense of being summoned, of a thread of awareness that seems to be calling to you. Mentally allow yourself to follow this call.

After a while, you will come to a "place" in the mind-scape that feels right to you. Allow yourself to remain in this place for a time. It may or may not have visual form, such as a meadow, or a comfortable home, or a place in space, or any other possibility you may imagine.

In time, allow yourself to begin to explore the place in which you find yourself. Simply explore, without judgment. Eventually, you will note that there are at least four distinct areas in this mental space which you have created/discovered:

An area of complete rest where you may safely and completely relax mind, body, and spirit;

An area to work where you may perform the tasks on the inner planes necessary to continue your journey on the outer;

An area to renew energy where you may tap into the infinite life-force of the Universe; and

An area to view outward that shows only truth.

The form these areas take is unique to you. Their character and the way they function will emerge from your inner nature. For some, there may be yet another area, a place where others may enter your sanctum but only with your permission. Take note of these areas. Come to know them, their essence. Remain relaxed. Breathe.

Continue to explore your sanctum. You may find that there are hidden places, some containing treasures, some containing horrors, all a part of the inner you, with which you must come to terms, as your journey continues. Remain relaxed. Breathe.

In the weeks, months, and years ahead, you will return to your sanctum many, many times. Your task is to build it in any image you wish. You may form and reform it in whatever manner you desire, using your powers of concentration and visualization. You may create sections to store knowledge, to study on the inner planes, to heal, and to function in other ways that you may need. In time, you may note that your sanctum has begun to shape itself according to your needs and development, even without conscious action on your part. It has become a part of you, changing and growing as you do.

This is your Inner Sanctum. It is yours, and yours alone. It is a place of refuge, of clarity, of rest and rejuvenation. A place to which you can retreat at any time. Soon, you will be able to find your way quickly and easily to this special private place. If necessary, in an instant, you may retreat to your sanctum, renew yourself, and return in the space of a breath. As you continue on your path, whatever it may be, allow this sanctum to remain with you as an inner resource. The many powerful uses for this profound tool will show themselves over the years, with further study.

YOGA

Choose anything but follow it to the source. The root is infinite, therefore the branch is also infinite.

Yehiel Mikhal Zlotchovi

The Yoga Systems

In the martial arts community, as with most disciplines that have a strong physical component, one of the most important developmental tools is supplemental training. That is using tools and techniques from outside sources to help improve one's abilities within the chosen discipline. In martial arts, the term for this is Hojo Undo (supplemental training).

There are many, many supplemental training methods used in martial arts and, indeed, they evolve over time as new concepts become available. However, some of the most well-known and respected are the various forms of Yoga.

Historically, the origins of many Asian martial arts are strongly rooted in India and the martial traditions developed there centuries ago. Tracing the evolution of

Chinese and even Japanese martial arts will show that, while all countries have their indigenous fighting styles, many of those that we think of today as Asian martial arts can be traced back to the Indian warrior castes.

Yoga means union, referring to the union of mind, body, and spirit with the greater All of the universe. Yoga has taken many forms over the centuries. What many think of today as Yoga, particular in the Western world, is a very limited view of true Yoga in its full scope.

Indeed, for many old-school yogi, martial arts practice is another form of Yoga. When you perform sequences of moves, going from one posture to another (kata), you are doing, what in Yoga is called *vinyasa,* transitioning from pose (asana) to pose. The actual transition process, the breathing and mental imagery or state, is just as important as the ending position. It would be entirely legitimate to say that, kata is vinyasa.

The interesting historical note for our purposes is that, in most cases, these Indian arts included, or were combined with, very deep mental and spiritual training methods. Thus, from their very beginnings, the physical and mental aspects of the martial ways were perceived and practiced as interrelated disciplines.

Of course, it is not the intention of this book to delineate all the many aspects of such a profound universe as that of Yoga. Whole libraries and all forms of media have been created on the subject. Here we will outline the basics of the various types of yoga methods.

The important point is to realize that all Yoga systems

are intended as paths to personal growth rather than merely physical development. While the physical benefits of yoga can be immensely useful to the martial artist, it is this mental/spiritual aspect which offers the greatest value and with which we are concerned here. As we look into traditional martial arts mental training methods we cannot do so without consideration of the very source of many of these concepts and techniques.

The primary forms of Yoga are:

Hatha
Laya
Raja
Bhakti
Jnana
Tantra
Kriya
Karma

Hatha Yoga (Yoga of the Physical Body)

Ha and Tha, the sun and moon, refer to the two opposite currents that regulate all processes in our body. There is nothing mysterious about it because everything in our universe exists because of a positive and negative charge. Hatha Yoga, Raja Yoga, and Kriya Yoga are specifically dealing with the intention of gaining control over the flow of these life-currents.

Hatha Yoga is known for the asanas or postures. It is thought that by perfecting the body, creating a healthy physical condition, and raising Kundalini (dormant energy) upwards along the spine, the body becomes better prepared for yogic awakening. The first effects felt are usually improved health and strengthened nervous system. Some Hatha Yogis may even demonstrate control over internal organs, blood flow, and breathing. The ability of some Yogis to even stop the breathing and heart beat completely for a period of time has been demonstrated under laboratory settings. Traditional Hatha Yoga consists of:

1. Asanas (postures);
2. Shat Karmas (six cleansing techniques, also known as Shat Kriyas);
3. Pranayama (control of breathing);
4. Bandhas (locks) and Mudras (seals) for the regulation of Prana (life-force) and Kundalini;
5. Samadhi (Union with God, realization of the Self, ecstasy, nirvana).

Laya Yoga (The Yoga of Energy Centers, Kundalini Yoga)

From Sanskrit, Laya means: dissolution; merging; in Yoga, absorption of breath and mind in the heart. Also called Kundalini Yoga, Laya is a practice whereby the Kundalini energy is raised, which is attainable through deep meditation (dhyana) and focus on the energy centers known as chakras. Laya Yoga helps the aspirant to attain union with the supreme consciousness. It is considered a complement to the physical practice of Hatha. If the body is not kept purified both externally and internally through the practices of Hatha Yoga, the succeeding steps of Laya Yoga would yield no result.

Raja Yoga (Yoga of Meditation, of the Mind)

Raja Yoga means royal and is sometimes called the crown of Hatha Yoga. Raja adds concentration after body and mind are cleaned and trained to stay calm and attentive. The improvement in our power of concentration, as a result of Raja Yoga, moves all of our attention towards the source of our Being in order to become that Being. Raja Yoga was sometimes referred to as Ashtanga Yoga because of the eight (ashta) limbs (anga) the system rests on. As of this writing, Ashtanga has come to mean a specific system of Asanas and mental disciplines rather than the original more generic meaning as relates to Raja Yoga. The Eight Limbs (Ashta-anga) are:

1. Restraints (yamas: harmlessness, truthfulness, non-stealing, control of senses)
2. Disciplines (niyamas: purification of body, mind and nervous system, study of metaphysical principles)
3. Postures (asanas)
4. Control of breathing and life-currents (pranayama)
5. Turning the attention within (pratyahara)
6. Concentration (dharana)
7. Meditation (dhyana: prolonged periods of perfect concentration and contemplation)
8. Spiritual Trance (Samadhi)

Bhakti Yoga (Union through Devotion and Love)

Bhakti Yoga is the Yoga of selfless love, compassion, humility, purity and the desire and serious intention to merge with the All.

Jnana Yoga (The Yoga of Knowledge)

Jnana Yoga is practical Philosophy/Metaphysics. It is both theory and practice. Jnana Yoga uses the intellect as a tool to understand that our true Self is beyond our mind. It is a Quest for the Self by direct inquiry into "who we are."

For the purpose of Self-discovery, Jnana Yoga probes the nature of the Self through the question: Who am I? Through persistent probing, fixing our attention on the source of our Being, we regain our real Self. We remember who we are. The inquiry, as the result of practicing Jnana Yoga, leads us towards clear Awareness by removing our attention from that which we are not. Along with Bhakti Yoga (Devotion), Jnana is considered one of the most powerful approaches to becoming aware of the eternal Self (All). Like Hatha and Raja Yogis, Jnana Yogis also acknowledge the relationship between breathing and thinking.

Tantra Yoga (The Yoga of Liberation)

The word tantra literally means "expansion." A tantra yogi concentrates on expanding all levels of his or her consciousness to unveil and realize the Supreme Reality. The tantric devotee strives to attune with the spiritual dynamic energy in order to transcend personal limitations and release subconscious blockages.

True Tantra Yoga is a pure path, but it has been abused by some self-proclaimed adherents. Tantra Yoga is not concerned with sexuality, but with the creative force and transmuting this energy into higher channels.

The goal of Tantra Yoga is to awaken and harmonize the Yin and Yang (Japanese, In and Yo) aspects within each person in order to spiritually awaken and realize the whole universe as an expression of the highest life force, or Spirit.

Kriya Yoga (Yoga of Spiritual Awareness)

Kriya Yoga refers to actions designed to rid the body and mind of obstructions. Kriya Yoga is a complete system including mantras, meditation, and other techniques aimed towards controlling the life-force and bringing calmness and control over body and mind. The goal is to unite with pure Awareness which is also Self-Awareness.

Karma Yoga (Selfless work for our fellow neighbor)

Karma is the total sum of all our actions (mental and physical), in this life and before. Karma Yoga is the yoga of Service or self-transcending Action, whereby the yogi directs all actions towards the greater good. By serving humanity without selfishness, egoism, and attachment the heart becomes pure, the ego fades and, over time, one becomes increasingly in tune and unified with the All. Enlightenment (Samadhi, nirvana, union) is naturally realized through long-term, consistent practice of Karma Yoga.

THE NEXT LEVEL

Knowledge is possibility. Knowledge in action is power.

JOL

Heiho/Hyoho (Strategy)

One of the most important aspects of the mental training of the budoka lies in the field of strategic thinking. For the martial artist, strategy is paramount. The application of martial techniques is completely dependent on good strategy in order to be effective in real situations. The advanced martial artist spends a good part of his or her energy learning various strategic concepts and developing tactics to apply those concepts. This is the case whether in sport, or life and death combat.

When you spend time around advanced martial practitioners, whether traditional or modern, you may notice a certain phenomenon. The closer the person's art is to reality, the more they talk about strategy. Those who train in arts where there is no resistance, hardly talk about strategy at all. As the realism level increases, so does the need for strategic and tactical thinking. When things reach the level of real world, life and death circumstances, strategy becomes paramount.

In time, this engenders a certain type of habit of thinking where one views every undertaking from a strategic perspective. In every part of life, the budoka tends to think and to act strategically, simply because s/he has learned to function this way. It is a powerful aspect of martial arts mental training and, ultimately, affects all aspects of life.

Our focus in this volume is specifically on strategic concepts from traditional martial arts. Clearly, there has been superb work on strategy from other sources and cultures. The reader is encouraged to explore these as well.

For those interested in studying ancient strategic concepts in depth, we must mention the most famous writings which every martial traditional martial artist should acquire. They are:

<u>Heiho Kadensho</u> – Hereditary Book on the Art of Swordsmanship by Yagyu Munenori
<u>Go Rin No Sho</u> – A Book of Five Rings by Miyamoto Musashi
<u>Bubishi</u> (Wubei Zhi) – Treatise on Armament and Combat edited by Mao Yuanyi
<u>The Art of War</u> – Sun Tzu
<u>Heiho Okugisho</u> – The Secrets of High Strategy by Yamamoto Kansuke
The Way and The Power by Frederick J. Lovret,

Strategic Concepts

The following is an overview of some examples of how strategy is taught in many traditional martial arts. In most cases, a teacher or mentor would guide the budoka in the choice of what strategies to study and tactics for their use. In other cases, an entire martial art might be built around a specific strategic doctrine. The student is then required to learn all the nuances of that strategy.

Here we just briefly touch on each of the concepts. No one would be expected to know them all beyond the basic ideas. A teacher might have a manual with these and many more, then choose which ones to teach based on the needs of the student(s). To explore any of them in depth can be a lifetime of study for each individual.

The important thing to realize is that integrating this kind of thinking into one's habitual mindset is a vital aspect of mental training for a budoka.

MAAI (Distancing)

Ranges

To-Ma (Far Distance - Kicking Range/Long Range)
Uchi-Ma (Striking Distance - Can strike with one step)
Chika-Ma (Close, Infighting Trapping/Grappling Range)
Uchi-Komi (Striking Step - Closing the Gap - Fitting In)

Nobashi no Heiho - Stretching out your opponent. Forcing them to attack from beyond their effective range.

Tokoshi no Heiho - To cross a great distance. Tactics to close the distance when you are at extended range.

Shikkotai no Heiho - Sticking close to your opponent like a coat of lacquer.

Nebari no Heiho - Binding your weapon (hands, sword, etc.) to your opponent's as they move.

Fukurami no Heiho - To expand your opponent. Taking your opponent's techniques outside of the sweet spot area(s).

Shukotai no Heiho - Fighting from a shorter range. Not allowing yourself to get extended/expanded.

HYOSHI (Timing)

Han'on no Heiho - Half-Step. Determine the timing of your opponent or create your own, then attack on the half-count (or any partial of the count). Note: Avoid having this done to you by training to use no discernible rhythm.

Katsuri no Heiho - Change speed. Force your opponent to fight in a rhythm, timing or pace that is unnatural.

Hitotsu no Tachi no Heiho - Sword of One. Using one strike as attack and defense. Sliding along the line of the attack and deflecting and attacking in one strike.

SUDORI (Passing)

Sudori no Heiho - Cause opponent to move, then when he or she is committed to a direction, change direction and counter.

Suigetsu no Heiho - Moon on Water. Evade and counter. e.g. small disengage, forward angle step, etc. Use evasion that takes advantage of opponent motion.

Irimi no Heiho - When opponent moves, step to his or her rear corner (Shikaku-blind spot) and attack.

Hito E Mi no Heiho - Weld, attach, bind yourself and opponent into one body. Then move with (In) or against (Yo), or at an angle, until you can take control.

Happo Biraki no Heiho - Open on all Eight Sides. Attack by Drawing (ABD) your opponent into your apparent open areas - requires Zanshin and Haragei.

Engetsu no Heiho - Full Moon. Expanding your size through posture or armor, to appear bigger, stronger, more dangerous, etc.

CHUSHIN (Centering)

Chushin Dori no Heiho - Taking the Center. - endless applications and variations.

Harai no Heiho - Clearing the Center (sweeping opponents 'sword' aside).

Hijiki no Heiho – 'Pressing' center then suddenly releasing to create an opening.

Momiji no Heiho - Softly, like a falling leaf, clearing center. Easy to say, hard to do.

Surige no Heiho - When frozen together, relax and enter, then lift, forcing an opening off center in any direction, leaving center unoccupied.

MINARI (Appearing)

Minari no Heiho - How you appear. Martial bearing, dress, face, reactions, etc.

Obiyakashi no Heiho - Threatening appearance. To threaten your opponent.

Utsurakashi no Heiho - Pretending to feel one way to lure your opponent into improper action.
Ryote no Heiho - Both hands: You can fight with a soft or hard strategy equally and can appear to intend one, then change to another.

*Kochiku no Heiho (*Tall bamboo) - The ability to bend, sway, appear one place then bend to appear somewhere else or as something else.

SENTE (Initiating)

Ichi no Hyoshi no Heiho - The Rhythm of One: Striking in a single breath. Without hesitation, step straight in and strike your opponent.

Munenmuso no Heiho - No mind, no thoughts, no plan.

Sekka no Heiho (Sekka: Spark from a flint) - Your technique is like a spark generated by your opponent's attack.

KAWARI (Changing)

Sankaikawari no Heiho - Mountain/Sea change: Your strategy is not working so you unexpectedly completely change what you are doing. The difference should be as the difference between the mountain and the sea.

Ryucho no Heiho – Bounce. A way of moving from one technique or strategy to another as well as resetting to help a technique work that has stalled.

Magiri no Heiho - Frequent, random seeming, small changes in strategy or technique.

Hanashi no Heiho - Letting go. When something doesn't work, immediately abandon it and try something else. Don't force it if it's not working.

Henka no Heiho - Variations on a technique or strategy, to adapt to the circumstances.

KAGE (Concealing)

Getsukage no Heiho - Moon Shadow. When you don't know what to do mirror or copy your opponent until an option appears.

Tachifumi no Heiho - To Stomp on a Sword. Aggressively shut down any attempt your opponent makes at attack.

Kageugokashi no Heiho - When you don't know your opponent's intention you must 'move the shadow' that's in the way using a *misekake* (feint) to make h/him reveal intentions.

Kageosae no Heiho - To Hold/Press Down a Shadow. Subtly move or act in such a way that opponent's moves are neutralized just as, or before, they can be applied.

Shinkage no Heiho - Spirit Shadow. Concealing your intentions either by using one technique to disguise another, or by not showing any clue, or 'tells' in face or body.

Metsuke no Heiho (Metsuke - The point where your eyes focus). Don't look directly at your opponent or their weapon. Have a more general focus which shows you everything while revealing nothing.

OJITE (Responding)

Nitobun no Heiho - Broken Rhythm Attack. Used against much stronger opponent.

Nagashi no Heiho – (Nagashi - to Flow). Flow with the opponent, especially if s/he moves well.

Zentai no Heiho - Total Body. Cut all parts of opponents body, from head to foot, including arms, or anything available, with one stroke of sword (or attack multiple parts of body simultaneously).

Menzuki no Heiho - Thrust to the face. Directly, possibly making him flinch, or overpowering, or out-speeding your opponent.

Kado no Heiho - Cutting a corner. If you can't get a major strike, take whatever you can get.

Kokorozuki no Heiho - Heart thrust. Focus on your true objective, even if your attack has been deflected.

OSAE (Controlling)

Makura Osae no Heiho - Holding Down a Pillow: Control opponent by restricting head motion.

Kuzushi no Heiho - Breaking Balance and Posture.

Shosotsu no Heiho - Think of opponent as one of your own men whom you can order around. Control opponent by making him do what you wish.

Hishigi no Heiho (Hishigi - Crushing) - The will to totally crush your enemy.

SUTEMI (Sacrificing)

Sutemi no Heiho - Sacrificing: The choice to sacrifice a small injury for a larger gain.
Aiuchi no Heiho - Mutual Kill: Strike your opponent at the same moment s/he strikes you.

KEIKAKU (Planning)

Daisho no Heiho - Large and small, Don't use a large sword to do a small sword's job; don't sweat the small stuff at the expense of the larger; conversely, don't lose sight of details while focusing on bigger picture.

Tateki no Heiho - Many Enemies. Your main concern is the order of battle. Not necessarily the closest opponent - but rather the most dangerous. The goal is either to create fear and disarray leading to disorganized and ineffective actions by your opponent, or you intention could be to set up a flow like a billiards shot.

Shidai no Heiho – Circumstances. You must be aware of, and use all factors, such as; environment, floor/ground, clothes, weapons, timing, physical and/or emotional conditions, defensibility/vulnerability, sight lines, etc.

Kaimon no Heiho - Opening the gate. If opponent is in strong defensive position use a strategy to create an opening or make him move.

PHILOSOPHY

The Sage walks a path constantly centered in the awareness of the All – living, breathing, eating, sleeping – beyond dogma or doctrine; constantly at one with the Way.

JOL

Dō & Jutsu

In Okinawan/Japanese martial arts you will come across an important distinction in how the arts are named. That distinction is between *Jutsu* (method), and *Dō* (pronounced "doe", meaning way or path). The basic concept is that any art can be practiced focusing primarily on the physical skills and techniques, which would be a *Jutsu*; or practiced as a path of personal, inner growth, as a Way of life, which would be a *Dō*. Thus, we have Aiki*jutsu* and Aiki*dō*, Ju*jutsu* and Ju*do*, etc. Both perspectives include some forms of mental training and many of the concepts and practices we describe apply to both. For the purposes of our present study of Seishin Shuyo, we will focus on the concept of Dō, (Chinese: Tao), the Way.

Dō (Tao) – The Way

The concept of a 'Way' as used in the martial arts, comes from the Chinese word Tao (Japanese: Dō) and translates as a "path," or "road," to higher levels of mental and spiritual awareness, knowledge, and wisdom, through commitment to the regular practice of a set of disciplines. Those disciplines form the bedrock of the road, or Path that one must walk.

The salient feature of a Way is that it is something you must physically do, not something you can simply think about or believe. It requires a conscious daily choice to act. The connotation here is one of a road or path that you follow step-by-step toward a goal which, in this case, is a lifestyle built on aiming for the highest levels of personal actualization.

A Way, or Dō, may be thought of as occupying the middle ground between religion on the one hand, and philosophy on the other. A religion is a specific unwavering doctrine that requires, first and foremost, the uncritical belief of its followers. You may accept the fundamental ideas of a particular religion without fully understanding - or even knowing(!) - all of its tenets. A philosophy, by contrast, can be a purely abstract, intellectual exercise. It may require nothing at all from you other than understanding its concepts.

When following a way, you aren't necessarily required to accept all of its principals without question, the way you must with a religion. Still, far more than philosophical exploration as an abstract, intellectual exercise *is* required. The key concept, the first principle which forms the very essence of a path, lies in the willingness to act. On a path, it doesn't matter how deep your knowledge, or sincere your belief, unless you actively and consistently *practice* those beliefs. You must take action each day in accord with the principles of whichever path you have chosen to follow.

A Dō is any discipline or philosophy actively practiced for the express purpose of the progressive development of the overall mental, physical, psychological, spiritual and social consciousness of the individual. A Dō, or Way, can take a myriad of forms. In fact, virtually any human endeavor can serve this role. There are as many Ways as there are people to follow them. The idea of a Way is an underlying concept which can be applied in an infinite variety of forms. It is this fluidity, in fact, that leads us to the second important feature of a Dō.

If the first principle of a Dō is action, the second principle lies in its flexibility and variability. A Dō is essentially a personal, individual exercise. The experience of following a Dō is an organic, fluid process continually evolving as the individual progresses. Thus, while a given Way may contain very specific concepts or disciplines, the nature of the practice of those disciplines may vary greatly from one individual to another.

This ability to conform itself to different individuals or even to different cultures without losing its essence is one of the most powerful aspects of a Dō (Chinese – Tao). It is infinitely variable, marvelously flexible, beyond any culture, time or place. A Dō can be adapted to fit virtually any circumstance. There are innumerable approaches to practicing its disciplines while remaining on the true Way.

Still, it must be understood that each Dō contains its own tenets, doctrines, and disciplines. In the beginning of the journey, the follower is constrained to adhere strictly to those principles with far greater commitment than many a religion or philosophy.

This commitment is, in fact, the third principle of a Dō. You can say you believe in a particular religion or philosophy, with those beliefs having little effect on your behavior. With a Dō this cannot be. The most vital aspect of following a Way is personal commitment. Belief without action is not the Way. You must "walk your talk." The commitment is to a conscious choice from day to day (truly, from moment to moment) to act in accord with the principles of your chosen Way. This level of commitment is the vital key without which there is no Way. The power of this commitment lies in the results of daily practice and in the fact that, in every moment, of every day you always have a choice of whether or not to act in accord with that commitment,.

Choice, then, can be said to be the final cornerstone of a Dō. Following a Way is always a matter of choice, both in terms of which "way" to follow and of each day's commitment to the disciplines. There is no "right" Way-only that which most deeply resonates within. Indeed, there is nothing stopping you from choosing to change from one Way to another.

Each of us seeks personal liberation. As we grow, we may find it is time to leave one road and take up another in order to continue our journey. This is in keeping with the heart of the Way. The important thing is the commitment to follow the principles of the teachings, whatever they may be, in our daily lives.

What becomes clear from all of this is the incredible scope that the concept of a Way encompasses. A Way allows for the full range of human activity and belief while still retaining a consistent set of underlying principles.

The essence of the concept of a Way, a Dō, lies in the four main ideas we've discussed:

Action - a Way is something one must do. It is not a set of ideas to be believed, but a process of discovery through study and practical experience;

Individuality - each of us, ultimately, must find his or her own way. A Way, once chosen, is an expression of individual experience. While every stage of the journey must be completed, the way in which this is accomplished is, ultimately, sourced from the individual;

Commitment - the key to following a Way is making the personal commitment to live by its principles. It is understood that any particular Way is only one of many equally valid possibilities. A given Way is chosen because the individual believes it can best serve his or her process of personal growth;

Choice - every moment of every day, you have a choice: to follow or not to follow the teachings of your chosen Way to the highest level of your understanding. This is the most powerful aspect of the Way as a means for the development of human consciousness, for it gives each of us responsibility for our own evolution.

There are many ways by which you may choose to live your life. Finding and following an appropriate Dō is only one of them. A Dō is a profound and powerful way to approach personal growth. Still, in the final analysis, it is only a road, a way. It is not the destination itself. The most insidious trap of following a Dō is becoming so immersed in its disciplines and practices that one loses sight of its original intent. The rituals and doctrine begin to overshadow the deeper purpose of the practice. Like a raft, built solidly so that one may safely cross a river, then gratefully, yet firmly, discarded once its purpose has been fulfilled, the Way must be seen for what it is: a road, a Tao, a Way to liberation - not liberation itself.

Zen

The relationship between the martial ways and the study and practice of Zen, or Zen Buddhism, is a long and storied one. An exploration in any depth at all is far beyond the scope of this volume. Numerous books, articles and other media have been created which feature the history, philosophy, primary people and interconnections between Zen and the various martial ways.

Zen is a practice based on the idea that the highest levels of inner development, often called 'enlightenment' can be actualized, through meditation and intuition, rather than following any particular religion. Zen also supports the idea that an activity such as martial arts practice, when approached as a method of meditation and sincere self-exploration, can lead to those same levels of development.

Beyond this, Zen philosophy focuses on ridding the self of ego and attachment to material things and to the varied circumstances of life itself. The concepts and disciplines that are a part of Zen practice have had a particular appeal to some systems of martial arts.

It is important to note however, that, while many budoka acknowledge and practice some forms of Zen, most others do not. For this volume, it is important to note that Zen can be a powerful form of mental training. In certain traditional martial arts, Zen philosophy has become completely integrated into the practice, while in others, it is not a part of the curriculum at all. In most, it is a matter of personal choice more than a specific requirement of the art. Zen philosophy and practice are subjects which the interested budoka might choose to explore to whatever level of interest, each in his or her own way and time.

HIGHER GROUND

Any sufficiently advanced technology is indistinguishable from magic.
Arthur C. Clarke

There have always been stories of mysterious, nearly magical abilities attributed to martial arts masters. In most cases, it is clear that these are the reports of observers not understanding what they were seeing. In any field it is possible for a committed person to attain such a high level of skill and knowledge that their abilities appear magical to the uninitiated.

With many years of practice it is possible for the serious budoka to develop levels of awareness and sensitivity that are far beyond the norm. However, we do not consider these a result of some mysterious metaphysical powers. Rather, they are the natural result of a lifetime of deep study and practice of the mental disciplines that should be part of the training of every budoka.

The following are some of the more esoteric mental skills that have been seen to emerge when one consistently practices Seishin Shuyo.

<u>Kan</u> (Intuitive Perception)

In the world of martial arts, indeed in any pursuit where life and death forms part of the stakes for which one is preparing, there is a very natural acceptance of the concept of intuitive perception. This is not viewed as something supernatural or mystical. Rather, this is simply a result of a life of intense training combined with circumstances that demand one's highest level of attention. This intuitive perception is known as Kan (感).

Author Dave Lowry writes in, 'Sword and Brush: The Spirit of the Martial Arts:'

"The concept of kan has particular importance for the bugeisha (budoka). Accustomed as he is to a keenness in his weaponry, he is naturally comfortable in extending the metaphor to his mental and emotional senses. This honing of the faculties of intuition begins as soon as his technical instruction starts,…"

The concept of Kan can take many forms, some of which are also well documented in the martial lexicon. These include: Dairok*kan* - or sixth sense; the quality of having a hunch or feeling about aspects of a person or situation that are not obvious on the surface; Kyo*kan* – the ability to understand and relate to others from their own perspective; and at the other extrememe, Satsui o *Kan*zuru – the ability to sense harmful or even murderous intent in another.

<u>Busai</u> (Martial Awareness)

Busai is the concept of always maintaining a clear sense of what is going on around you. In modern terms this might be similar to what is called situational awareness. The distinction however, is that Busai, similar to Kan, also includes an element of intuitively sensing danger, or at least its potential.

Some of this is a simple matter of conscious choices such as where you walk or sit in public, noticing the people around you, and leaving any situation that seems uncomfortable. It is the unconscious combining of a number of clues along with trusting one's feelings.

However, another element of Busai is known as Ryochi no Hakken (intuitive knowledge). This is considered to be a more pure intuitive knowledge that emerges when one engages in particularly arduous and austere training (shugyo).

Haragei (Belly Knowledge)

Yet another form of intuitive awareness, Haragei is much more direct and powerful. Haragei is specifically related to knowledge and feeling related to another person. It can be an exchange of feelings and even thoughts. It can be knowledge acquired while engaged in contest or combat or it can be sensing when one is the subject of intense focus. Haragei is the faculty that allows you to sense in advance the moves of your opponent.

Haragei can also be viewed as a form of charisma, a powerful quality of presence which can be felt by those around you. Hara, the belly, is the source of Chi, the internal force that resides in all living things. The power of one's life force can be so strong that all around you can feel it as you move through everyday life. This quality of personal power can be seen in many long-time budoka.

<u>*Kiai and Aiki*</u> (Spirit Meeting, Harmonious Spirit)

"Aiki is an impassive state of mind without a blind side, slackness, evil intention, or fear. There is no difference between aiki and kiai; however, if compared, when expressed dynamically aiki is called ki-ai, and when expressed statically, it is aiki." 'Jiu-jitsu Kyoju-sho Ryu no Maki, Textbook of Jiu-Jitsu'

"The most profound and mysterious art in the world is the art of aiki. This is the secret principle of all martial arts in Japan. One who masters it can be an unparalleled martial genius." from the 'Budo Hiketsu-Aiki no Jutsu, The Secret of Budo,' 1899

"Aikido training without kiai does not make big progress. It is not powerful and has no energy. With a big kiai, a training is full of energy. That is why it is better to shout out loud. O'Sensei (Aikido founder Morihei Uyeshiba) always said, 'What kind of kiai is that? Make a bigger kiai! Go outside and let the sparrows fall from the trees!'" Sensei Morihiro Saito

In the Japanese and Chinese view of the Universe there is a concept known as Ki (気) (Japanese: pronounced, kee), or Chi (Qi)(Chinese: pronounced, chee), which can be translated as internal or intrinsic energy. That is the fundamental life force that is a part of all living things.

Obviously, a book such as this cannot even begin to explore the full scope of this term. Many, many volumes have been written about Ki (Chi) in many languages and from virtually every perspective. However, the basic concept of Ki is vitally important as relates to Seishin Shuyo. In that context, there are two relevant, and interrelated concepts to consider.

The term Ai (合) can be translated variously as, unifying, blending, harmony, meeting, connecting, joining, etc., depending on the context. In the martial ways we combine the terms in two ways. One way is the word Kiai and the other is the reversal of the parts to for the word, Aiki. These two terms, Kiai and Aiki can be seen as the Yin and Yang (Japanese: In and Yo) of each other. Just as Yin and Yang are depicted by one circle containing both dark and light, Kiai and Aiki are connected in a continuous flow. And just as the dark portion of the Yin/Yang circle (the Yin portion) contains a small seed of Yang, and vice versa, Kiai and Aiki each contains the seed of the other.

Most people think of Kiai as the 'spirit shout,' the loud yell you often hear during Karate or Kendo practice and which refers to uniting all of one's mental, physical and spiritual energies into the moment of the strike. Aiki, on the other hand, is more often perceived as related to the arts of Aikido and Aikijujtsu, where the unifying, or blending is thought to be concerned with blending, or harmonizing with, and then redirecting the energy of an opponent. However, these, like most concepts in martial arts, comprise only the surface view.

Developed through fukushiki-kokyu (deep abdominal breathing) along with other martial disciplines, both Kiai and Aiki, as aspects of mental training, form a major part of the heart and soul of the true expression of martial arts in action. It is the union of all that one has, as well as the ability to sense, relate with, and flow with everything your opponent brings. The ability to do this spontaneously, in the most extreme moment is a part of what truly defines the budoka at the highest level.

Shu-Ha-Ri (Obey, Break, Transcend)

Among the many concepts of mental training in martial arts, there is a model of the learning and growth process known as Shu-Ha-Ri. These are thought of as stages along the path to the highest level of expression of your art.

Shu translates as, 'obey,' 'maintain,' 'protect,' or 'keep.' It implies accepting and practicing exactly what you are taught without many questions. It is all about doing your best to imitate what you are shown as exactly as possible and absorbing the techniques and concepts the way they are taught. In Okinawan/Japanese arts, this stage would last a minimum of 10 years. Indeed, many find complete satisfaction at this level for their entire lifetime in the arts.

Ha means, 'to break,' or 'detach.' In martial arts circles, it implies that, after a long period of developing a solid foundation in knowledge and technique, you may begin looking more critically at what you have learned, breaking down and re-arranging, or even changing certain things to fit your personal attributes or needs. This is often a very long period of serious introspection and experimentation, easily 20 - 30 years or longer and, more often than not, any changes made can be very subtle and personal rather than large in scale.

Ri, has many interpretations including; to leave or depart, transcend or go beyond. The concept of Ri implies breaking away from the set forms of a system and, either creating your own forms or, at the highest level, reacting completely naturally without the constraints of any particular form or method.

Aikido Master, Shihan Endo Seishiro writes:

"It is known that, when we learn or train in something, we pass through the stages of shu, ha, *and* ri. *These stages are explained as follows. In* shu, *we repeat the forms and discipline ourselves so that our bodies absorb the forms that our forebears created. We remain faithful to these forms with no deviation. Next, in the stage of* ha, *once we have disciplined ourselves to acquire the forms and movements, we make innovations. In this process the forms may be broken and discarded. Finally, in* ri, *we completely depart from the forms, open the door to creative technique, and arrive in a place where we act in accordance with what our heart/ mind desires, unhindered while not overstepping laws"*

Sifu Dr. Yang Jwing Ming states: *"It's the student's job, after they learn the essence from their teacher, to develop the art and change the art to fit their own body. Basic patterns are the same, basic structures are the same. But it will always be slightly different for each person. It's meant to be. Everything is relative. It depends on the person and the situation. You have to keep your mind open. One thing is for sure, if you are doing everything precisely like your teacher after you have practiced for thirty years, you missed the point."*

While in some martial arts circles there is strong resistance to the idea of changing anything from the way it was originally taught, in other circles this idea is accepted as quite normal. In those disciplines, one is expected to develop a personal approach just as in any other art form such as, painting, music, etc., where one first imitates the masters but, after a time, is encouraged eventually to develop h/his own style or sound.

Many believe that adapting to time and circumstance is, in fact, more traditional than not doing so. In times when one's art is used for life and death, one must always adapt to changes in weaponry, techniques and tactics of the opponent. Every combatant always wants the latest and best in equipment, weapons and skills. This is the only way to survive when the stakes are at the highest possible level. Budoka who don't adapt, die. Arts that don't adapt, eventually wither on the vine of lost relevance.

The same may apply to the mind of the budoka. The essential point of the path is to continue to grow as a person. Part of that process is making your art your own by cultivating the mentality of adapting it to your needs and circumstances.

Takemusu (Spontaneous Creativity)

Takemusu is a term used by Aikido founder Morihei Ueshiba. It means infinitely generating or creating in the moment, without plan or preconception. Takemusu is beyond adherence to any particular system or structure. It is pure creation in accord with one's nature and perfectly in harmony with the needs of the situation. The mentality of Takemusu is such that one might never repeat a particular technique, and certainly never perform it the same way twice. Each moment is unique and the perfect choice of technique, strategy, tactic and application can only be created in that moment. Ueshiba is said to have considered this the highest level of the art.

Kenshō (A Moment of Enlightenment)

Kensho is a term from Zen, and has been studied in great depth by many scholars of philosophy. We must say however, that Kenshō is an *experience* rather than something one learns merely academically. It has been described in a wide variety of ways, likely because the experience can be so different for each person, and so difficult to put into words.

Ken (見), translates as "seeing," while shō means "nature" or "essence." Thus, a Kenshō is a glimpse into the deepest nature and/or meaning of anything, from a single technique, to the vastness of the Universe. Often the insights are related to a higher understanding of the self, to seeing one's true nature.

The experience of Kenshō can be very short, lasting

seconds or moments, or much longer, lasting days or even weeks. However, though the effects can last a lifetime, Kenshō is not viewed as a permanent enlightenment, or Satori. Rather it a glimpse, a peek into pure essence.

Kenshō is not considered to be a single experience. Rather it is part of a process, an ongoing, continually upward spiraling series of realizations and insights which continue throughout life. For the budoka, the experience of Kenshō is an integral, expected, and welcome result of the consistent practice of all the physical and mental martial disciplines of the martial ways.

Shibui/Shibumi (The Touch of Grace)

This word can have multiple meanings depending on the Kanji and the context. For the mental training of the budoka, we are referring to shibui, which translates as elegance, grace, or refinement, yet in an understated, unpretentious way. Shibui is a combination of the highest level of quality, yet with no elaboration or flashiness. It is the quality of something being precisely what it is, no more or less, but with great hidden depth under a simple, unadorned appearance.

One way that shibui is expressed in traditional martial arts is with the uniform, which is almost always, simple, white or black and unadorned with anything more than, perhaps, the crest of the school or style. The simplicity of this uniform is intentional as it represents a clean, simple, yet elegant appearance, containing an art, and a person of extraordinary depth and scope. The budoka seeks to bring this attribute not only into the habits of thought, but also into daily life. Thus, you many find the most advanced practitioners living in a way that is relatively ordinary, quiet and unassuming while containing many layers of richness, love, joy, sharing, learning, and growing. This is the heart of Seishin Shuyo as expressed through the day-to-day life of the budoka.

THE WARRIOR ARCHETYPE AS METAPHOR

To the warrior is given the duty of unrelenting discipline of mind, body, and spirit. The warrior metaphor teaches us all of the lessons required for dealing with our daily lives. Through the practice of the arts and ways of the warrior, we develop an iron will and an indomitable Spirit.

Of the many images, the wide variety of icons we might choose to emulate in our quest for personal actualization, that of the warrior is one of the most powerful. The Warrior represents, as much or more than any other archetype, the quintessential doer - "...to know and to act are one." This is a fundamental axiom of the Warrior credo - s/he must "walk the walk" rather than merely talk the talk.

This is the first and most fundamental requirement for anyone who chooses a path as their way of going through life. As we have discussed, the first stage on the path requires that you take action, to live day-to-day in accord with its principles and practices. No image more clearly embodies the path of action than the Warrior. Everything in the training and education of the Warrior is based on the premise that s/he will someday have to use that training, to act on it in life-threatening situations. To do so reliably, repeatedly, in the face of great adversity, requires qualities of heart, of will, of physical and mental strength and endurance that are unique.

The beauty and power of the Warrior as metaphor, however, lies not only in the attributes themselves, but in the training that develops them. This is where the Warrior archetype has the most to offer us on our quest.

It may be that, of all the ancient archetypes, the Warrior is the one where the steps necessary to the actualization of the required qualities are most clearly outlined. Sadly, we humans have engaged in violent and aggressive behavior toward one another since time immemorial. In so doing, we have developed reliable methods to turn our young into very effective soldiers.

The value of this is that the very same training can be used to develop the mental attributes required of the committed seeker of self-actualization. Rather than focusing on violence and destruction, the same qualities of endurance, courage, loyalty, perseverance, skill, dedication, attention to detail, service to the greater good, and many others can be harnessed to serve on your personal journey.

Any path is long and hard and the temptation to surrender, to give up and move on to an easier way of life, is very strong. Who better to prepare us to endure this journey than the Warrior, whose whole life and training is oriented toward just that end? Never to surrender, no matter the difficulty or danger, never to give up, but to endure, to keep going forward till the objective is achieved, is the most basic tenet of the warrior code.

The very same tools and training methods that have evolved over, literally, thousands of years to train such discipline, commitment and endurance with the intent to destroy, can now serve to transform. This is one of the aspects of warrior training that has long been noted. The training methods and lifestyle, the challenges and experiences, the pain, the fear, the fatigue and need to face yourself, to acknowledge your strengths and overcome your weakness are a part of all warrior paths. Properly implemented, the experience changes the practitioner permanently. These methods are well-known and reliable. They can be used for good or ill, but they always work.

Bushi (The Warrior)
Hallmark - *Endurance*
Highest Duty - *To Serve*
Challenge - *To Face Death*
Attainment - *Mastery of Fear*

The Hallmark of the Warrior is Endurance.

This is the sine qua non of the Warrior way, the most fundamental and most recognizable of the Warrior attributes and applies, not only physically, but mentally as well. From the most common soldier to the greatest of spiritual knights, the very first lesson that any-and everyone who chooses to undertake warrior training must learn, is to endure. Without this utterly vital capacity, fully developed in mind, body, and spirit, the warrior is certainly doomed to fail - to die.

For one who chooses to follow a Way of any kind, no attribute can be more necessary, or more welcome. The reality of the day-to-day challenges to one who follows a path are such that, without the Warrior's hallmark – endurance - one simply cannot see the journey through.

For the Budoka, this is truer than for most. The Way of the Budoka is essentially a choice of commitment and discipline, throughout your entire lifetime, to study and training. While there are many necessary attributes, those who pursue the Budoka Way must assimilate this first, most basic trait deep into their bones, into their blood, into the very essence of their being. Without the capacity to endure the long journey, to meet every challenge with the unwavering belief that, regardless of all else, you will never quit, you are entering battle unarmed.

This is one of the primary reasons the "basic training" of the soldier has evolved into the forms we see today. Centuries of hard lessons have taught the necessity for this lesson to be drilled deeply into the psyche of the warrior trainee. The path of the Warrior, the daily hardship, the life-and-death struggle is such that nothing less than virtually limitless endurance will suffice to see the soldier through. Budoka physical and mental training reflects this ideal.

The Highest Duty of the Warrior is To Serve.

In every ancient tradition, service is considered one of the highest forms of expression of personal commitment. To act with the intent to serve the needs of others is a fundamental aspect of higher consciousness, and an integral facet of the practice of the Budoka lifeway.

Service, of course, may take many forms. The Warrior, who has attained a high degree of personal power through his or her training, offers to use that power in service to his or her community. The Warrior willingly places him or herself between society and the forces that may endanger it. This act may sometimes be quite literal, as in military, law enforcement, fire service, search and rescue - or in other, not so physical forms such as political or social activism. In any case, the Warrior takes up the battle for those who cannot do so themselves and, in so doing, faces the hardships and dangers inherent in such acts of courage.

This process engenders many qualities conducive to personal growth. There is no greater testing ground for the body, mind, or spirit than battle. If the Warrior can maintain personal integrity through truly selfless service, regardless of the outcome or reward, and often without even the appreciation of those he or she serves, then a deep, unassailable awareness of self can emerge. This sense of personal inner strength will serve the Warrior, or the follower of any path, throughout the journey to self-actualization. In essence, by giving service, it is ultimately the Warrior who is served.

The Challenge of the Warrior is to Face Death.

The ultimate act of courage is to consciously and willingly face the possibility, even the certainty, of one's own death, and still act with integrity. This is the true challenge of all who walk the Warrior path. Do not, however, construe this to be concerned only with physical courage, for this is not our meaning at all. Physical courage is admirable, to be certain. However, it is also the heart and mind with which we must concern ourselves. This is the battlefield on which the greatest victories and defeats, the most heroic acts of courage and the most craven acts of cowardice, will occur.

Every living entity fights to continue its existence. This is true, not only of those we normally think of as living, but also of all parts of the human psyche - those that serve us and are conducive to our growth and welfare, as well as those that do not and are not. One of the most difficult parts of the journey is to face the aspects of ourselves that dis-serve us, and take up the sword of discipline and commitment to engage these enemies of personal evolution in battle, with the implacable will never to stop until they are not only defeated, but utterly dead - in effect, to kill parts of our very selves. For many, this is not merely difficult, but impossible. However it is precisely this that the Budoka intends: to seek out and destroy those enemies of self-actualization which lie deep within all of us.

The concept of death in all its many aspects is an intimate acquaintance of the true follower of the Warrior ways. S/he lives with death as a constant companion, and comes to know its many forms and guises. In time, the Warrior comes to a deep acceptance of his or her personal relationship with death - not in a morbid or fatalistic way, but rather in a centered understanding of its essence. *"The Way of the Samurai is found in Death… If, by setting one's heart right every morning and evening, one is able to live as though his body were already dead, he gains freedom in the Way. His whole life will be without blame and he will succeed in his calling."* Yamamoto Tsunemoto – 'Hagakure – The Book of the Samurai'

<u>*The Attainment of the Warrior is Mastery of Fear.*</u>

"Fear is the mind killer. Fear is the little death that brings total obliteration. I will face my fear. I will permit it to pass over me and through me. And when it has gone past I will turn the inner eye to see its path. Where the fear has gone there will be nothing. Only I will remain."

Frank Herbert,
Dune

The greatest impediment to accomplishment, to the attainment of success, to the fulfillment of dreams, is fear. Fear runs so deeply in the human psyche that, in one way or another, it can affect every choice and action. The sources, the scope and range of our fears are, quite obviously, one of the most serious subjects in the study of human psychology and can hardly be adequately addressed here. Rather, we may touch briefly upon the effect of the practice of the Warrior way in regard to fear.

The Warrior arts require, as much as anything else, that we face ourselves - that we learn, on the deepest and most visceral level, certain fundamental truths about our nature. We must then find ways to act in accord with our highest understanding of the principles by which we have chosen to live, regardless of the fears that such actions may evoke. In the practice of the soldierly arts, this obviously entails facing the threat of death or injury and still doing one's duty. In the case of the Warrior path, this means facing all of the "slings and arrows of outrageous fortune" with integrity.

The Budoka does not attempt to eliminate fear. We accept it as fundamental to human nature. Rather, through the study and practice of the Warrior disciplines, we seek mastery of the effects of fear upon our thoughts, choices, and actions. It is the Warrior arts that, through long experience, have most effectively developed clear and effective methods to deal with this most debilitating of emotions. In time, the Warrior may reach a stage where fear is transcended, transmuted into power, and where the Warrior ceases to live a life bounded, caged by primordial fears. Emotions which no longer serve a true survival purpose but rather inhibit the process of evolution of consciousness can be transmuted into tools that serve the actualization of our true capabilities.

Bushi no Kokoro (The Warrior's Heart)

The Warrior archetype contains many powerful and valuable attributes. Historically, we only need look at such warrior societies as the Knights Templar, the Samurai, the Sundancer, the Zulu, or any of a wide variety of others to find numerous attributes such as loyalty, courage, integrity, discipline, and perseverance. Clearly, these assert themselves in many forms. Nor are we so naïve as to believe that all members of these groups were exemplars of the benevolent warrior. Still, the qualities and training methods of the Warrior undeniably offer many powerful and effective tools for those who would follow any path. It is the manner in which those tools are employed that determines their ultimate value to ourselves and our community.

For the martial artist, the study of the warrior arts and disciplines forms the backbone of our practice. The attributes of the Warrior teach us not only the lessons necessary for continued progress on our journey toward self-actualization, but also for dealing with our daily lives. It is through the forge of intense warrior training that the profound strength of will, of heart, and of mind intrinsic to the Warrior way is deeply ingrained in the budoka. These attributes become the source on which we rely, both in our daily practice and in the times of great difficulty that are sure to be encountered in life.

MARTIAL MAXIMS

Absorb what is useful. Discard what is useless. Add what is specifically your own.

Bruce Lee

The martial arts world is notorious for being filled with hundreds, perhaps even thousands of little sayings, or maxims, intended to teach various concepts and principles. The subjects of theses maxims can range across the full gamut of issues that relate to the martial path. Volumes have been written cataloguing many of these. Here we'll take look at just a few that apply specifically to the mental aspects of the path, although, in some ways all of the martial maxims can be said to be a part of the mental training of a budoka.

Dojo Kun

Dojo Kun are the sayings recited by the members in many Okinawan/Japanese based martial arts schools at the end of group classes. They are intended to express fundamental philosophical principle which the practitioner will carry not only during training but in daily life as well. This is one the most overt forms of Seishin Shuyo that you will find in many martial arts schools. Here are some typical Dojo Kun from a few well known arts. Often, they are recited in Japanese then in the language of the school's participants. Here I have used the English translation. Of course, there are many, many more:

Shotokan Karate

- *One: Strive for the completion and perfection of one's character*
- *One: Be Faithful and protect the way of truth*
- *One: Endeavor – Foster the spirit of effort*
- *One: Respect others and the rules of etiquette*
- *One: Refrain from violent behavior (guard against impetuous courage)*

Goju Ryu

- *One: Be humble and polite*
- *One: Train considering your physical strength*
- *One: Practice earnestly with creativity*
- *One: Be calm and swift*
- *One: Take care of your health*
- *Live a plain life*
- *Do not be too proud or modest*
- *Continue your training with patience*

Ryu-te

- *Strive for good moral character*
- *Keep an honest and sincere way*
- *Cultivate perseverance through a will for striving*

- *Develop a respectful attitude*
- *Restrain physical aggression through spiritual attainment*

Shorinjiryu Kenkokan Karate

- *Maintain propriety, etiquette, dignity and grace*
- *Gain self-understanding by tasting the true meaning of combat*
- *Search for pure principle of being: truth, justice, beauty*
- *Exercise a positive personality: confidence, courage and determination*
- *Always seek to develop the character further, aiming towards perfection and complete harmony with creation*

Ju no Kage Ryu Kenpo

- *Never give up*
- *Always do your best*
- *Strong practice equals strong karate*
- *Always show respect*

More Maxims

- *The ultimate aim of karate lies not in victory of defeat but in the perfection of the character of its participants.*
- *Iki Sho Ten (Will and energy will lift you up)*
- *Ichi I Senshin (Focus everything on a single goal)*
- *Shin Gi Tai (Unite your mind, technique and body)*
- *The focused mind can pierce through stone.*
- *Exert oneself in the perfection of character.*
- *Be faithful and sincere.*

- *Cultivate the spirit of perseverance.*
- *Be respectful and courteous.*
- *Refrain from impetuous and violent behavior.*
- *A warrior is one who sees his or her truth and then dares to live it.*
- *Make the warrior walk your everyday walk.*
- *Make Perfection your goal and excellence your standard.*
- *Relax and calm your mind. Forget about yourself and focus on the movements of your opponent.*
- *Defeat is a state of mind.*
- *Adversity is a mirror that reveals one's true self.*
- *Let neither anger or fear find lodging in your mind.*
- *Quiet your body, quiet your mind.*
- *Feel your confidence and see yourself winning. Always see yourself winning.*
- *As a human being one should train one's mind and one's ability to the fullest.*
- *Sword and mind must be united.*
- *Subjecting yourself to vigorous training is more for the sake of forging a resolute spirit than it is for developing a strong body.*
- *Mental bearing, calmness, not skill, is the sign of a matured warrior.*

- ❖ *When you find your inner peace through meditation, you can carry it everywhere with every waking moment, even into war.*
- ❖ *Inner mental technique is more important than the physical one.*
- ❖ *You must concentrate and consecrate yourself wholly to each day, as though a fire were raging in your hair.*
- ❖ *A negative frame of mind runs counter to the principle of maximum efficiency.*
- ❖ *A black belt is a white belt who never quit.*
- ❖ *If the spirit is strong, one will appear like a deep, flowing river, calm on the surface, but with tremendous power hidden in the depths.*
- ❖ *It is difficult to understand the Universe if you study just one planet.*
- ❖ *Foster and polish the warrior spirit while serving in the world; illuminate the path according to your inner light.*
- ❖ *A thousand days is just to forge the spirit. Ten thousand days is to polish what you forged.*
- ❖ *Fear is a great servant but a terrible master*
- ❖ *Spirit first, technique second.*
- ❖ *It's not the size of the dog in the fight, it's the size of the fight in the dog.*

- *Winners constantly think in terms of, "I can, I will, I am."*
- *We must first set our hearts right.*
- *Human beings, by changing the inner attitudes of their minds, can change the outer aspects of their lives.*

SEISHIN SHUYO

It remains for me to point out the great advantages conferred by the knowledge of this doctrine.

Baruch de Spinoza

There is little doubt that the incredible power of the mind is the key factor to attainment in every aspect of life. It's not unreasonable to assert that every great achievement is built, to some degree, on various aspects of mental capability.

There are many other facets of the martial arts that have not been covered here. Some of those could arguably be included under the rubric of mental training. Certainly readers may ask why I have not covered such well-known subjects as Bushido – the famous Samurai code of behavior, or the myriad great books that have been written on various other facets of martial life, including, not only training and strategy but philosophy, ethics and even aesthetics. Many of these subjects are integral parts of the budoka lifestyle, and hopefully we can look at some of them in subsequent volumes.

Clearly, there is also a very large body of modern information regarding all aspects of the relationship of the mind to high performance. Such techniques and devices are extremely powerful and effective. They are simply not the subject of this work.

The budo, traditional martial ways, are unique in that, not only are the various types of mental abilities clearly delineated, but the path to development of these mental powers is very well defined. By studying and practicing the disciplines of Seishin Shuyo you have a sure road to follow toward actualization of your true capabilities.

By consistently practicing the Kihon (Basics) over time, the mental qualities of calmness, centeredness, clarity, openness, compassion, balance, and strength of will begin to emerge in your everyday life. Persevering, fighting and winning spirit are tempered though the practice and development of the many minds. The strategic approach to all endeavors becomes second nature. In time, by living the martial way daily, one begins to exhibit the fundamental hallmarks of the budoka: endurance, service, and eventually, mastery of fear.

The heart of the Budoka Way lies in practice of the many disciplines, physical and mental, that comprise this ancient path. The road is long, and the requirements demand the most that you have to give.

Fortunately, along with the demands, the traditional martial arts offer the tools needed to remain on the path. These tools serve in every part of life and remain permanently valuable and useful. It is my sincere hope that, through this writing, you have become aware of one of the most important, and powerful tools the martial arts and ways have to offer - that is Seishin Shuyo, Mental Training.

ABOUT THE AUTHOR

Jimmy Lockett began martial arts practice in 1967 with Judo under Mr. Harold King. In 1969 he began studying Kenpo Self-Defense (Shorei Kenpo Goshin Jutsu), a combination of Okinawan and Chinese Kenpo Karate, under Master Herman Griffin. Jimmy remained with Master Griffin until the master's death in 1998. Jimmy also wrestled on his high school team for three years and practiced boxing with his brother, a 1976 Olympic alternate. He began studying Yang Style Tai Chi Chuan in 1985 and Jujutsu arts in 1987.

Jimmy has studied 5 Animals Kung Fu with Art Sykes, Aikido with Dusty Young and James Noriega, Small Circle Jiu Jitsu with Wally Jay, Gracie Jiu Jitsu with Reylson Gracie, Jeet Kune Do Grappling with Larry Harsell, Daito Ryu Aikijujutsu Kodokai and Hakuho Kai in NYC, and Muso Shinden Eishin Ryu Iaido under S. T. Khan in NYC. In 1987, Jimmy began practicing Filipino Kali/Escrima through Master Dan Inosanto.

Jimmy has been a certified Aerobics instructor and personal trainer, certified Herbalist, certified in Ohashiatsu and Do-In Shiatsu, and a licensed paramedic (NREMT-P).

Jimmy is a member of United Martial Arts Alliance International (UMAAI), and a Life Member of the United States Martial Arts Federation (USMAF), the United States Ju Jitsu Federation (USJJF), and USA-Traditional Kodokan Judo (USA-TKJ).

Jimmy holds the title of Kyoshi, and the ranks of 7th Dan in Okinawan/Chinese Kenpo Karate and 5th Dan in Moritakan Ryu Jiu Jitsu. The system he has developed, Ju no Kage Ryu (Ten Shadows Style) Kenpo, is recognized as an official martial art style by the USMAF and the USJJF.

Made in the USA
Middletown, DE
05 March 2018